SEPTIC TANKS
and Aqua-privies from Ferrocement

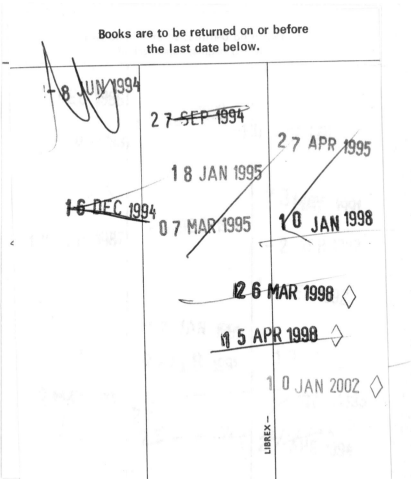

Intermediate Technology Publications Ltd., 9 King Street,
London WC2E 8HW, UK.

© Intermediate Technology Publications 1984

ISBN 0 903031 95 7

Printed by the Russell Press Ltd., Bertrand Russell House, Gamble Street,
Nottingham NG7 4ET.

Contents

List of Figures

Tables

Acknowledgements

The author and the publishers would like to thank Arnold Pacey, for skilful editing; Barry Lloyd, John Pickford and Ian Goldman for their detailed comments on the text and their constructive advice; and John Collett, ITDG Water Programme Officer, for co-ordinating the progress of the project.

Preface

This handbook is a contribution to the steadily increasing literature on low-cost sanitation. It describes a ferrocement septic tank especially designed for sewage disposal at isolated sites in Britain. The design is also widely applicable for the markets of Europe and North America, where this handbook should be of direct practical use. Ferrocement tanks are also highly appropriate to many situations in developing countries because their manufacture requires almost no capital equipment. The handbook therefore discusses the possible uses of ferrocement septic tanks for improving sanitation in low-income communities, and briefly indicates the modifications in design which may be necessary in these circumstances.

The publication is written for public health engineers, planners and field-workers engaged in improving sanitation both in developing countries and in the industrialised world. Although some acquaintance with sanitation technology is assumed, the material is presented in non-technical language to a very large extent. The handbook has three chapters:

Chapter 1 describes the potential of ferrocement as a construction material. It then describes the range of applications for which septic tanks and related techniques such as aqua-privies are used, and reviews the scope for ferrocement septic tanks across the world.

Chapter 2 gives details of how septic tank and aqua-privy waste treatment and soil disposal systems are designed and constructed. The complexity of the physical, chemical and biochemical processes in waste treatment are emphasized to show how design has ultimately to rely on specification.

Chapter 3 gives step-by-step construction details of a ferrocement septic tank built for the commercial market in North Wales in the British Isles. The information and specifications given here will be readily adaptable for the design and construction of aqua-privies also.

Ferrocement is a proven low cost, less capital-intensive structural material. The design and construction methods given in this handbook will, it is hoped, indicate the potential of the material for sanitation development.

CHAPTER ONE

Applications of Ferrocement Septic Tanks (and Aqua-privies)

1 ADVANTAGES OF FERROCEMENT TANKS

Septic tanks made from ferrocement have been successfully used in many parts of the world. Built of a shell of cement mortar, reinforced with wire strands and mesh, their construction is mainly carried out by hand. They are easy to make and a manufacturing operation is cheap to set up.

The thin shell of the tank is built into a curve and has great strength and flexibility. Because the mortar is worked by hand a dense material is produced that is durable and able to resist the corrosion of even the most concentrated sewage likely to be experienced in domestic installations. Ferrocement has the following advantages over other materials used to build prefabricated septic tanks in developing countries:

(a) Commonly available materials are used

The basic raw materials of water, sand, cement and reinforcing wire are likely to be readily available in most areas. The other materials described, used in the construction and curing work, are needed in small quantities only, and should not prove prohibitively expensive.

(b) Skills

The basic skills involved in the construction work are plastering and wire-tying, which may be learnt by an unskilled person in a few weeks' practice. Supervision is generally left in the hands of the tank builders themselves. The work is essentially labour intensive.

(c) Simple equipment

The basic formwork needed for construction is relatively cheap to make and easy to repair. The hand tools themselves are also cheap and widely employed in building work everywhere. A motor-powered concrete mixer eases the labour of construction considerably.

(d) Diverse products

Ferrocement is used to make a very wide variety of thin shell structural products, from cattle troughs to buildings, and is becoming increasingly popular all over the world. A construction yard specializing in ferrocement work will therefore not restrict its product range to septic tanks.

The main disadvantage of ferrocement tanks is their weight. It is usually best to prefabricate them in a builder's yard, but then a vehicle and lifting tackle are needed to move each completed tank to its site.

The particular design of septic tank whose construction is described in the latter part of this handbook was designed initially for the commercial market in rural districts of North Wales, in Britain. However, the design requires little modification for use elsewhere; and the essential features of its construction are also applicable to aqua-privy tanks. The purpose of this chapter, then, is to review the conditions in which septic tanks and aqua-privies of any kind may be most appropriately used, and then at the end of the chapter to return to the question of ferrocement construction. Detailed instructions for constructing the tank are given in Chapter 3, which complements the author's earlier publication *Ferrocement Water Tanks* (Watt, 1978); this should be consulted for a more comprehensive guide to ferrocement.

2 WORKING PRINCIPLES AND HEALTH ASPECTS

The septic tank system and the aqua-privy use the same basic principle for waste treatment and disposal. Both depend on holding sewage in an enclosed tank to allow some solids to settle and decompose through the process of digestion. With both systems, also, a constant volume of sewage is retained, so fresh inflows of wastes are compensated by the outflow of a liquid effluent. The latter consists of water with some solids carried in suspension, as well as other substances produced during the digestion process carried in solution, and is usually disposed of via a soakaway in the soil. The solids that accumulate as a sludge in the bottom of the tank must be removed periodically as they build up, so as to maintain the required volume for settlement.

The safe use of a soakaway depends on the suitability of the soil. Any householder contemplating installation of a septic tank will therefore need to check carefully that he has sufficient land for its satisfactory operation, and he will need to examine soil and water-table conditions according to the criteria which are described in Chapter 2. The point to note here is that the effluent from septic tanks is, from a health standpoint, almost as dangerous as raw sewage, and should on no account be discharged into surface drains or streams without further treatment.

The main function of a septic tank, therefore, in either an aqua-privy or a septic tank system, is to separate and digest the solid constituents of sewage. Some disease-causing organisms (pathogens) may be trapped in the tank, particularly the larger parasite eggs which may settle with the solid matter. Some organisms may be killed by conditions within the tank. But it should be clearly understood that these processes do not provide complete or reliable treatment. The effluent from the tank is therefore likely to carry many of the pathogens that were present in the original sewage.

Tank design can be modified in various ways to reduce the health hazards associated with the effluent. A feature in some septic tanks, and some aqua-privies, is that a partition divides → the tank into two compartments. Raw sewage enters the first compartment and effluent leaves the second. The effectiveness of this arrangement can be further improved if it is possible to avoid diluting or stirring up the sewage in the first compartment with sudden, high-volume flows of used washing water (sullage).

Another factor which affects the quality of the effluent is tank capacity, because in general, the longer the time during which the sewage is allowed to digest and settle, the more

3

disease-causing organisms will die, and the more parasite eggs will sink to the bottom. One Chinese septic tank system allows for up to 20 days retention of sewage in each compartment, with generally good results, but this requires tanks that are much larger than would be practicable in most circumstances.

Because of the hazards associated with septic tank effluents, it is recommended that *soakaways* should be located at least 30 metres from any well or stream, and at least 3 metres from any building. The septic tank itself should be 1.5 metres from buildings, and 10 metres from streams and wells. Thus considerable areas of land may be needed for the safe operation of a tank and soakaway system. Septic tanks and aqua-privies are for this reason unsuited to medium-density and high-density urban areas, except in special circumstances where sewers can be used to carry away effluent, or where secondary treatment of effluent is possible (as discussed in Chapter 2). Instances will be mentioned later of specialized adaptations of septic tanks for use in congested slum areas, but in nearly all such cases, unusual and carefully planned arrangements are made for the discharge of effluent and for the periodic desludging of the tanks. Extreme caution should be exercised with all urban installations; many cities in tropical countries experience major health problems because of the use of septic tanks without adequate effluent disposal, where surface ponding occurs.

3 OPTIONS FOR SANITATION TECHNOLOGY

The relevance and applicability of septic tanks in the world today can best be understood by briefly reviewing other sanitation options. These range from the simplest pit latrines, as are used in rural areas of developing countries, to the costly sewerage systems that are the norm in western cities. Many recent books have examined the economic, technical and health aspects of these various technologies, among them, an important World Bank series on 'appropriate technology' for sanitation (see World Bank, 1980, particularly, 1980a, b).

A basic distinction is made in this series between sanitation

4

techniques which can be used independently by individual households, and systems which depend on the services and infrastructure of a large community. This leads to a classification of sanitation options such as that presented in Table 1. It will be seen that the basic ferrocement technology described here for the septic tank is relevant to several of the options listed, though some of these are relatively specialised applications.

Septic tanks serving individual households (item 5 in Table 1) are perhaps most typical of high-income western societies, though increasingly also of residential areas in Africa and Asia. In North America, there are some 17 million septic tanks serving households whose total population amounts to 54 million. Tank designs which have evolved to serve this market are based on the assumption that families have cistern-flushed latrines located within their homes, and that large volumes of water are used for bathing, washing, laundry and cooking. This entails a relatively expensive septic tank installation with a large soakaway and with drains

Table 1. A summary of sanitation options.

A. Household sanitation technologies

1. Pit latrines
2. Pour-flush latrines with soakage pits (Figure 2)
*3. Pour-flush latrines with septic tanks
*4. Pour-flush aqua-privies (Figure 1)
*5. Cistern-flushed latrines with septic tanks
6. Composting latrines

B. Community sanitation technologies

7. Bucket latrines with hand-cart collection
*8. Latrines with vaults and vacuum-cart collection
9. Communal facilities using bucket latrines or vaults
*10. Communal facilities discharging to septic tanks or aqua-privies (Figures 3 and 4)
11. Communal facilities connected to sewers
12. Individual cistern-flushed latrines connected to sewers.

*indicates the possible applicability of ferrocement construction.

serving several points within the house.

In developing countries, by contrast, we are sometimes concerned with aqua-privies, or more often with various other types of pour-flush latrine (items 2-4 in Table 1). In all these options, pipe-work is simpler and soakaways have to deal with only small volumes of water, so costs can be much lower and less land is required. It is therefore of interest to examine the applicability of aqua-privies and other types of pour-flush latrine in a little more detail.

Figure 1. Basic aqua-privy.

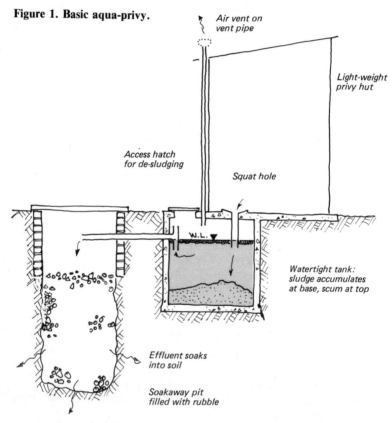

The principle of the aqua-privy. The water level in the tank needs to be kept at the level marked 'W.L.' by adding water daily. Many different kinds of soakaway can be used to deal with the effluent from the tank. The soakaway shown here consists of a pit filled with broken stones.

Figure 2. Pour-flush latrine.

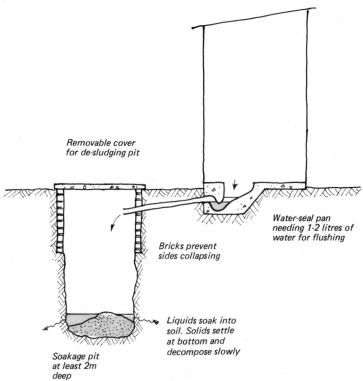

Removable cover
for de-sludging pit

Bricks prevent
sides collapsing

Water-seal pan
needing 1-2 litres of
water for flushing

Liquids soak into
soil. Solids settle
at bottom and
decompose slowly

Soakage pit
at least 2m
deep

The distinctive feature of the aqua-privy is that it consists of a latrine mounted immediately above a small septic tank (Figure 1). It is typically sited in a back-yard, a short distance from the house whose occupants it serves. Despite its cost-saving features, however, it is rarely as cheap to construct as a pour-flush latrine connected directly to a soakaway (Figure 2), and the latter has the additional advantage that it can be installed inside the family house, if that is desired. This latter type of latrine is widely used in India, and in recent years has often been emphasized as a widely applicable technique.

Efficient sanitation for low-income communities presents enormous problems going far beyond the scope of this book, and where planners or field workers with wide responsibilities have to make a choice, all the options listed in Table 1 may need to be examined. The World Bank documents quoted above provide the most detailed available assistance in making choices of this sort, most notably through a series of very helpful algorithms or flow charts of the decisions to be made.

Here there is space only to sketch out the circumstances in which decision-makers may favour septic tanks and aqua-privies, and we have noted that, as technologies for use by individual households, they are generally too costly to be considered for very low-income groups. There may, however, be circumstances in which a septic tank can economically form part of a communal system, with one tank possibly serving as many as 200 people (item 10 in Table 1).

The most straightforward applications of the latter kind are septic tanks which serve latrines in a rural school or hospital. However, septic tanks and aqua-privies of specialized design have been successfully used to meet sanitation needs in city slums and congested refugee camps. One especially novel example, in which the two compartments of the conventional septic tank are replaced by two pillow-shaped butyl rubber bags, is the Oxfam sanitation unit (Figure 3), a design which often has more than four steps. Designed for short-term use in refugee camps, several of these units have successfully functioned in Bangladesh for over two years, and more than four years in some other areas, each unit serving as many as 1,000 people.

Novel types of aqua-privy, designed for more permanent use in city slums have been developed in Bangladesh, India (Calcutta) and Nigeria (Ibadan). The Bangladesh design has the aqua-privy tank above ground level, with access to the latrine via four or five steps; this makes it possible to desludge the tank by gravity flow. All these latrines are designed either for communal operation, or for shared use by large extended families. Under these circumstances, and with suitable precautions for safe disposal of effluent, aqua-privies can be appropriate to the needs of the urban poor, and can be installed at relatively low cost.

There is one further point to be made about the use of septic tanks in developing countries which relates to their high cost when installed at individual homes. Although this

8

Figure 3. The Oxfam Sanitation Unit.

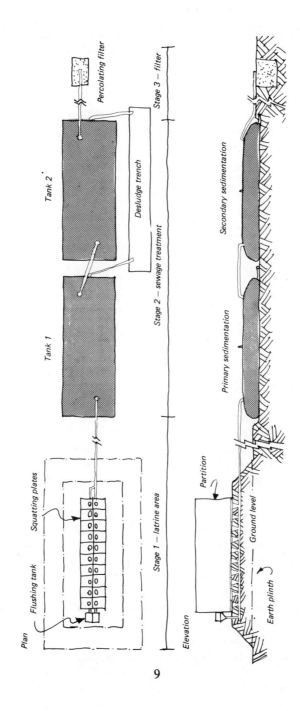

The Oxfam Sanitation Unit. A communal latrine is shown to the left of this diagram. Effluent from the two pillow-shaped tanks is discharged via the percolating filter to the right. (Courtesy of Oxfam)

9

might make them seem totally inappropriate, especially in the context of cities noted for slums and shanty towns, all such cities include more prosperous communities. If septic tanks are not available as an option for the better-off families with suburban homes, these people will often demand the installation of conventional sewerage. This is a charge on public funds, and tends to divert resources away from low-cost sanitation for low-income groups.

The World Bank recommendation, therefore, is that the construction of septic tanks at *private* expense should be encouraged in many places as an alternative to *public* expenditure on waterborne sewerage. Thus septic tanks are an important sanitation option in that they can be constructed without commitment of community funds: "as part of a sanitation package that can meet the needs . . . of all the members in a given community, septic tanks have a widespread potential . . ." (World Bank, 1980, p.7).

4 COST CRITERIA AND WATER SUPPLIES

One problem with the operation of aqua-privies is how to ensure that sufficient water flows into the tank for it to operate as it should. In the most common designs, the latrine consists of a squat hole with a vertical drop pipe, down which users' excreta fall directly into the septic tank.

As long as the water level in the tank is maintained so that the lower end of the drop pipe is submerged (as in Figure 1), this arrangement works well, without undue smell and without attracting flies. The problem is that, to keep up the water level, users must pour one or two buckets of water into the tank daily. In practice, this is rarely done, either because users are unaware of its necessity, or because they dislike the labour of carrying water into the toilet.

The result all too often is that water seals are not maintained, smells develop, and the tank attracts flies and mosquitoes. One country in southern Africa banned the construction of aqua-privies for this reason. Experience has been better in Islamic countries and in parts of India, because where people use water for anal cleaning, they will usually take sufficient water into the privy with them as a matter of course.

The so-called self-topping aqua-privy is sometimes built to overcome this problem in places where there is a piped water supply. In this system, waste water from washing or other activities enters the tank and ensures that the correct water level is held. However, this additional water necessitates a more extensive soakaway or a large soakage pit and so more land is required. The dilemma therefore is that self-topping aqua-privies cannot be used in urban areas, or where soils are unsuitable for soakaways: but the simpler aqua-privy shown in Figure 1 presents such problems concerning its water seal that most authorities now tend to discourage it.

Apart from these limitations on the applicability of aqua-privies, the cost of making and ensuring a water-tight tank has to be considered, and the additional costs of a self-topping type are a major factor. Thus the World Bank documents quoted above argue strongly that the aqua-privy cannot be recommended as a viable sanitation option. Instead, they emphasize a simpler pour-flush latrine (Figure 2) as a lower cost alternative. This has a water-seal pan and discharges into a soakage pit without need for a water-tight tank.

World Bank data on comparative costs underlines the disadvantages of the aqua-privy. Low-cost options such as pit latrines, composting latrines and pour-flush toilets of the type shown in Figure 2 can all be built for a total investment per household of *less than 400 U.S. dollars* (at 1978 prices). This assumes that each household has its own individual latrines, and in some instances, costs may be as low as 70 dollars per unit. By contrast, investment costs for other options are as follows (World Bank, 1980):

Aqua-privy, 1,100 dollars per household;

Septic tank, 1,645 dollars per household;

Conventional sewerage, 1,480 dollars per household.

Because water is so crucial to the operation of a septic tank or aqua-privy, it is relevant to look at the applicability of

11

various sanitation options in relation to the type of water supply available to the household. Three levels of water supply are indicated in Table 2, which points to the fact that septic tanks are limited to households with piped water, whereas related technologies such as pour-flush latrines require only that water is available nearby, from a backyard tap or pump.

Before we complete this general review of the application and use of septic tanks, it is worth noting one specialized type developed in China with the particular aim of allowing effluent and sludge to be used as liquid fertilizer. Considerable health hazards would normally be involved in this, and to reduce these as far as possible, a very large septic tank system is constructed, in which sewage can be allowed to stand for many days. Given sufficient time, many pathogens will die.

The use of the effluent as fertilizer also requires an additional storage tank into which effluent can be discharged and held until such time as it is appropriate to use it on the land. The addition of this storage facility has led to the development of what is called the 'three-compartment' septic tank (Figure 4). Because of the large size required, however, each compartment is constructed as a separate tank. The first two compartments function in a similar way to any other septic tank, with a constant water level. But the third compartment, which is larger than the others, fills up as effluent is discharged. Periodically, it is emptied by scooping liquid out through a hatch in its cover, but during this operation, the water level in the other two compartments is maintained.

The capacities of the first two compartments are fixed with the aim of giving a 10-20 day retention time. The third compartment has a 30 day retention time, and is emptied at approximately three-week intervals.

Some doubt may be cast on the adequacy of the treatment provided in this type of installation; even with long retention times, the fertilizer has a significant health hazard, but much depends on local conditions. In rural China, these tanks are certainly a vast improvement on the techniques used previously, and are used to treat animal excreta as well as

12

Figure 4. Three-compartment septic tank used in rural China.

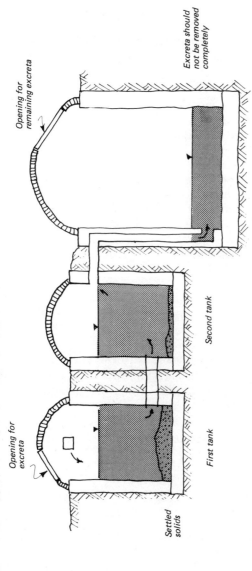

Opening for excreta

Opening for remaining excreta

Excreta should not be removed completely

Storage tank

Second tank

First tank

Settled solids

Sewage enters the system on the left, and liquid fertilizer is scooped out of the storage tank on the right using buckets. The two tanks on the left of the diagram function as a conventional two-compartment septic tank with a fixed water level. They are typically 1.5 metres deep, and vary in diameter, according to the number of people using the system, from 1.3 to 2.0 metres. The other dimensions marked are in centimetres.

(From a report by the Epidemic Prevention Stations of the districts of Chinkiang and Chiong, Province of Kiangsu. Reproduced by courtesy of the International Development Research Centre, Canada.)

13

Level of water service	Household sanitation options		
	low cost	medium cost	high cost
All water carried by hand from a distant source	pit latrine or composting latrine	n.a.	n.a.
Yard tap or pump owned by household	pit latrine or composting latrine	aqua-privy or pour-flush latrine	n.a.
			n.a.
Water piped into house	composting latrine	pour-flush latrine in the house discharging to septic tank	cistern-flushed latrine in the house discharging to septic tank or sewer

night-soil collected from bucket latrines. They are also used with pour-flush latrines discharging directly into them, often in situations where a communal toilet serving many people can feed into one septic tank.

An alternative design, widely used in China, is to utilize the digestion process to generate and collect methane for use as fuel (see ITDG, 1979).

5 RANGE OF APPLICATIONS FOR FERROCEMENT TANKS

It will be obvious from what has been said in previous paragraphs that aqua-privy tanks are normally much smaller than septic tanks. They have to deal with very much lower volumes of waste water, and are not normally used with cistern-flushed latrines. However, the differences in tank

14

capacity are not very great, and the problems involved in redesigning the ferrocement septic tank described in Chapter 3 for use as an aqua-privy are not insuperable.

A detailed discussion of how tank sizes should be judged according to the number of people using the latrines is presented in Chapter 2. Suffice it to say here that aqua-privy tanks serving family groups vary in capacity from a recommended minimum of 1,000 litres below the water line, up to 1,800 litres. By contrast, septic tanks serving individual households in the United States vary in capacity from 2,000 litres up to 4,500 litres, while septic tanks serving institutions have a minimum size, in America, of about 3,500 litres, and may more typically be 10,000 litres in size and more (USDHEW, 1959, pp.31 and 49).

In developing countries, small septic tanks may be appropriate to take the discharge from pour-flush latrines. Such tanks provide a better means of sewage disposal than the simple soakage pit shown in Figure 2, but for a latrine of the same type without a cistern flush. Tanks used in these circumstances should have a minimum capacity of 1,500 litres below the water line, and larger capacities will be required according to the number of users and the amount of waste water or sullage being dealt with.

The ferrocement tank described in this handbook has a capacity of around 4,000 litres and is therefore very suitable for the majority of household septic tank systems. Redesigned to about half this size, it would correspond well with the capacity of aqua-privy tanks being built in Calcutta for extended family groups (see Maitra, 1978). In this connection, it is worth noting that although the use of aqua-privies is now strongly discouraged by the World Bank and by other government and academic experts, the aqua-privy is a very well-established type of latrine, and will certainly continue to be used in some places. In Calcutta, some 30,000 are reported to be in use in conditions where the pour-flush latrine described above would not be satisfactory. The ferrocement tank could be modified for use as an aqua-privy relatively easily be redesigning the tank cover to incorporate a squat-hole and drop-pipe (or water-seal pan, according to local practice).

Table 3. The range of applications for which ferrocement tanks may be used in sanitation.

Context	Application	Design
1. rural areas in Europe and North America	septic tanks for isolated households	as described in Chapter 3
2. high-income, low-density suburbs in cities in developing countries	septic tanks as an alternative to sewerage for homes with piped water	as described in Chapter 3
3. schools, hospitals, and communal latrines in developing or developed countries	septic tanks serving groups of latrines	the tank described in Chapter 3 may be used, in multiple for large installations, or larger ferrocement tanks may be designed.
4. rural and low-density urban areas in developing countries	small septic tanks used with pour-flush latrines	tank described in Chapter 3 redesigned to smaller capacity
5. rural areas and, with precautions, some urban areas in developing countries	aqua-privies for individual households with backyard taps or pumps	ferrocement tank redesigned to smaller capacity and with aqua-privy fittings
6. urban areas with vacuum trucks for sewage collection	latrines with vaults in individual houses	ferrocement tank designed to specifications of local sanitation authority

One further application for which ferrocement tanks are also sometimes used is as household vaults or sewage holding tanks in cities where sewage is collected and carried to an off-site disposal facility by vacuum trucks (option 8 in Table 1). Such systems are fairly widespread in eastern Asia, and especially in parts of Japan. It will be apparent, then, that ferrocement tanks of the same basic construction can be used for a variety of sanitation options. Table 3 summarizes the wide range of these potential applications.

CHAPTER TWO

Design Principles for Septic Tanks and Aqua-privies

1 INTRODUCTION

This chapter describes in detail the design and operation of septic tanks and aqua-privies and the disposal of their effluent into soakage beds or pits in the ground. Secondary methods of treatment to improve the quality of the effluent and lengthen the life of the soakaways are also described.

Each element of septic tank and aqua-privy systems is described to show how it works and the factors that affect its performance. Recommendations are made on the detailed design of the system, most of them based on careful studies made by the WEDC Group in the Department of Civil Engineering, Loughborough University of Technology.

2 FACTORS AFFECTING SEWAGE TREATMENT EFFICIENCIES IN THE SYSTEMS

There is a considerable amount of uncertainty about the detailed functioning of most septic tank systems, leading to a degree of uncertainty in design. One reason for this is that in small-scale plant, such as septic tanks and aqua-privies, there is not a steady flow of incoming sewage. There are surges and shock flows which expose the tanks to wide variations in sewage flow and strength, which disturb the treatment processes. Efficiency of waste treatment therefore varies, and effluent quality varies also. Large tanks tend to smooth out these variations, but extra tank capacity has to be paid for. Poor quality effluent can be improved by secondary methods of treatment before it is discharged for disposal into the soil. In order to analyse this problem of effluent quality, therefore, we need first to consider the quantity and strength of sewage inflows into septic tanks, and then consider the options for secondary treatment of the effluent, or for its natural improvement during percolation through the soil.

(a) Sewage inflow — quantity and strength

Sewage quantity. Domestic sewage may contain excreta, water used for washing the body, clothes and dishes, and kitchen wastes. Raw faeces contain roughly one part in four solids, but diluted domestic sewage may contain less than one part in four thousand solids. Septic tanks are normally designed to handle all liquid wastes, whereas aqua privies usually take just excreta and flushing water; septic tanks are therefore larger and require greatly increased areas of soakaway to dispose of the effluent.

The daily quantities of sewage to be treated will depend on the number of people using the system and their habits of water use. Generally, water usage increases with standard of living. In Europe and North America, where piped water is plentiful and households have multiple taps, liquid wastes can reach 600 litres/person/day, although 200 l/p/d is more normal. In developing countries, where water is carried from standpipes, liquid wastes are unlikely to exceed 40 l/p/d. There are clearly many ways to economize in water use that will also reduce the volumes that have to be disposed of.

Aqua-privies require a minimum of about 20 litres of water added daily to keep them topped up and the water seal intact; the actual volume used depends on the ready availability of water supplies and the flushing habits of the users. The aqua privy pan, if it is not flushed clean after use, will become fouled and encourage insects and flies; at least 1 litre per defecation may be needed for flushing — more if the surface is rough. The volume needed for flushing excreta from a water-sealed pan to a septic tank depends on the design of the W.C. pan itself; water usage can often be cut many times without affecting flushing ability.

There is a strong case to be made for separating faecally contaminated wastes (black wastes) from washing water (grey wastes) as this reduces the effluent load from the tank which is still highly charged with pathogens. In this case the relatively unpolluted 'grey' wastes are passed through a small

19

settling tank to remove grease and grits and/or discharged directly to the soil. The separate soakaway area for the 'black' wastes will as a result be very much smaller with less risk of soil blockage and surface flooding. The aqua-privy is usually designed to deal with 'black' wastes only, leaving 'grey' wastes to be disposed of separately, though self-topping aqua-privies take a limited amount of waste water from both houses or showers. Rainwater drainage should never be passed through a septic tank or aqua-privy.

Sewage strength. Domestic sewage strength depends on its dilution and whether or not 'black' and 'grey' wastes are mixed. Its strength will depend initially on the solid and dissolved matter in the sewage.

Water from body washing will contain small amounts of body grease, dirt and soap; kitchen wastes contain soap, waste food, some grit, and straining water from food preparation; and excreta itself contains highly complex organic compounds with a heavy charge of micro-organisms. The solid matter may float, sink or stay in suspension; the dissolved matter may consist of organic or inorganic compounds.

The daily weight of faeces per person to be treated depends on diet, ranging from 200-600 grams for people on a high carbohydrate or vegetable diet; this is more than three times the weight of faeces compared with people on a high protein or meat diet. To the weight of excreta must be added the weight of materials used for anal cleansing — which may be considerable, plus weight of urine. These values will vary widely between individuals of different ages in the same community.

The strength of sewage is conventionally measured by two parameters: first, the amount of oxygen needed by micro-organisms to oxidize nutrients in one litre of sewage — its 'Biochemical Oxygen Demand', or BOD — and secondly, its suspended solids content, or SS — the weight of filterable material per litre of sewage. Many other parameters are also used, among them nitrogen content, pH, bacteria count. The strength of a sewage to be treated varies constantly and does not allow the treatment processes in the tank to reach a steady state condition. However, the total daily input of solids into a septic tank is more or less stable with most family installations and can be used as a design parameter.

(b) Treatment processes in the tank

Both septic tanks and aqua-privies are simple reservoirs that still the incoming sewage allowing the solids time to settle and in time be partially digested. Treatment in the tank is a complex interaction of physical, chemical and biochemical processes that are not easy to isolate from each other (Figure 5).

In a full-size sewage works, settling tanks have a retention time of up to two and a half hours, removing 50-70 per cent of suspended solids and 25-40 per cent of BOD; high rate purpose-built sludge digestors which are heated and stirred have retention times of 10-20 days and are used to mineralize and stabilize already thickened sludges. In contrast, septic tanks and aqua privies have retention times of 1-3 days, BOD removal may be less than 50 per cent in cold climates and up to 75 per cent in tropical climates; solids dilution varies greatly and the solids themselves are likely to be in larger, more discrete fragments — especially in the aqua-privies.

Septic tanks and aqua-privies combine settlement and digestion in the same tank, which interferes with the efficiency of both processes.

Settlement of solids. The still conditions in the tank allow solids more dense than water to settle to the bottom of the tank as sludge, the rate of settling depending on the density of the particles. Lighter particles, oils and greases float to the surface to form a scum layer which effectively keeps the stored sewage completely airless, or anaerobic. Between the sludge and scum layers is a body of clear sewage called 'supernatant liquor' which carries small colloidal particles in suspension; these may coagulate to rise or fall according to their density. Coagulation is encouraged by gas bubbles from the digesting sludge rising up to the surface — a process which can also disturb the settlement of solids. Settlement itself is faster when the sewage is warmer and less viscous.

The perfect settling basin carries the incoming sewage

21

evenly along to the outlet and allows the solids time to settle without disturbance, the heaviest particles falling fastest. In practice this is impossible to achieve and incoming sewage surges cause turbulence and eddies that carry settling solids and even sludge up to the surface. If the basin is poorly designed the incoming sewage may even short-circuit the basin and flow out with hardly any settlement of solids taking place.

Figure 5. Treatment processes in tank.

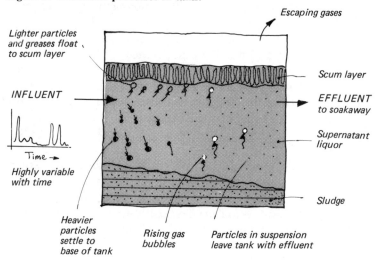

Digestion of solids. This is essentially a two-stage process carried out by different groups of bacteria. In the first stage the organic matter is fermented, broken down and liquified to produce, amongst other compounds, foul-smelling volatile fatty acids; these acids are in turn used by methanogenic bacteria to produce gases and water. Other organic compounds are produced as by-products. Efficient digestion requires vigorous mixing to bring the bacteria into contact with their various foods, but this would interfere with the settling process. Digestion is therefore slow and incomplete in the sludge and scum layers. Some stabilization of the supernatant liquid will take place during its passage through the tank.

Rising bubbles of gas carry particles of sludge up to the scum layer; these particles may help coagulation of the colloids or they may be washed out of the tank to increase the effluent strength and decrease its quality.

Digestion is also temperature-dependent, the bacteria increasing in activity as temperature increases, reaching a maximum at 35°C. Few tanks reach these temperatures, although they may be approached in tropical climates; in cold climates tank temperatures fall and in the winter months little digestion of solids will take place at all.

Methanogenic bacteria are highly sensitive and are affected by overloading that produces too much acid, by toxic substances and by large temperature changes. On the other hand tanks may be left for long periods without any sewage loading, and the bacteria remain dormant; digestion recommences after sewage is again loaded in. During storage, sludge is compressed due to the weight of the top layers and may become so compact that de-sludging by suction pump is impossible.

The efficiency of treatment processes in the tank therefore depend on a wide variety of factors, not only on sewage characteristics but also on tank design and operation. Effluent quality will vary greatly throughout the day and average effluent parameter values over long periods have little meaning; some typical values of septic tank efficiencies are given in Table 4. A few massive surges that wash out solids may block an otherwise satisfactory soakage field; surges in septic tanks will be reduced by a long delivery pipe. In aqua-privies they are unlikely to occur unless large volumes of water are used for flushing or are washed into the privy.

Effect on micro-organisms. Many different species of micro-organism exist in working septic tanks and take part in the digestion processes. To start up a new tank, it is often necessary to take sludge from a working tank with a 'balanced' population and transfer it to the new one.

Micro-organisms that are found in human excreta generally find the environment of the tank hostile. Some sink

Table 4. Examples of effluent quality in septic tank and aqua-privy systems (WEDC, 1979).

Determination	Brandes	Salvato	Barshied & El-Baroudi	Ottis & Boyle	Robeck et al	Viraraghvan
Year and location	1977-Canada	—	1974-USA	1976-USA	—	1973-Canada
Number of tanks	1	—	20	6	—	1
pH	7.9	7.4	7.14	—	7.5-8.1	6.95
Alkalinity ($CaCo_3$)	667.8	400	227	—	400	—
Total solids (TS)	596.7	820	390	—	46	215
Suspended solids (SS)	81	101	39	54	36	117
BOD_5	143	140	223	159	90	295
TOC	76	—	—	—	—	91
COD	—	—	452	360	—	556
Ammonia (N)	131	12	40	39	22	93
Nitrites	0.02	0.001	—	—	0.008	—
Nitrates	0.16	0.12	—	—	0.11	0.013
Total phosphate (P)	20	—	8	15	—	11
Orthophosphate	17	—	8	12	—	—
Chloride	100	80	—	—	75	53
Total coliforms No./100ml	0.2×10^6	—	—	—	5×10^6	6×10^6
Faecal coliforms No./100ml	0.11×10^6	—	—	0.42×10^6	—	1×10^6

Note: All data is given in mg/l.

to the sludge layer with the organic solids and some swim freely. The proportion of them destroyed in the tank depend on the species and time of retention in the tank — the longer the retention the greater proportion destroyed. Tank effluent may be expected to contain large numbers of viruses, bacteria, protozoa and helminths that are still infectious; tank effluent and sludge must be treated with great care if the spread of disease is to be avoided.

(c) Secondary treatment processes

The tank removes solids from the sewage to prevent them clogging the soil surfaces in the soakaway. Further treatment prior to disposal to clarify the effluent can be carried out through a number of secondary treatment processes (Figure 6). Each of these also involves a complex interaction of physical, chemical and biochemical processes, and each could justify a chapter on its own. For some the performance control methods have been well tried and tested for nearly a century; for others, observation has hardly begun. In practice, these secondary methods of treatment are rarely used with small domestic tanks, but they may be of the utmost importance where septic tanks are used in urban situations in which an adequate soakaway cannot be constructed.

Biological filters or bacteria beds are common in both large and small sewage treatment works (Figure 6a). They consist of a ventilated, well-drained bed of a suitable medium, such as large gravel through which effluent is trickled from distribution devices. This surface becomes colonized by a thin film of micro-organisms of varied species that absorb solid and dissolved organic matter from the effluent and convert it into cell mass. When the layer of micro-organisms becomes too thick it sloughs off and is washed down to be collected in a second settling tank — where it is pumped up regularly for disposal or to the septic tank for digestion.

Effluent from biological filters can achieve high chemical standards although it still contains many pathogens. The filters need regular maintenance and the final settling tank needs regular de-sludging; if neglected the media will clog up,

25

and if allowed to dry out, the micro-organism population dies. They can cause fly and odour nuisances. Filters are expensive to construct and are only appropriate for the larger installations where the site is located on sloping ground, and where an effluent of a standard suitable for discharge into a water course is needed.

Anaerobic up-flow filters or 'Bank's clarifiers' consist of a coarse screen on which anaerobic bacteria fasten themselves to absorb both dissolved and organic materials from the effluent. A loose flocculent mat is built up which further acts to strain out solids and provide a living environment for the bacteria (Figure 6b).

Up-flow filters or clarifiers are common in large sewage treatment works where controlled flows are passed up through a simple wire mesh screen. For smaller works with their effluent of varying quality and flow rate, the screen must have a large surface area for the bacteria to grow on, and a gravel layer is more appropriate which can be simply back-washed by hosing down from above when the tank is de-sludged.

Observations on working tanks suggest up-flow filters can improve effluent BOD and suspended solids quality by up to 70 per cent. Improved designs use a combination of clarifier and sand filter but these need more frequent back-washing.

Up-flow filters would seem to have great potential as a cheap effective method of improving effluent quality but there has been little comprehensive research work carried out or practical experience that can be used as a basis for design.

Sand filters are sometimes incorporated in the final disposal system and are passive devices that need to be cleaned by removing and washing the sand when blocked up. They may be constructed to pond the effluent with underdrains below the sand to collect the filtered effluent; or mounded up around tile drains to allow vegetation to grow and use the chemicals in the effluent as food and reduce the soakage load by evapo-transpiration (Figure 6c).

Filters may be expected to improve effluent BOD and suspended solids by as much as 95 per cent; they are very

Figure 6. Secondary treatment processes.

(a) Biological filter.

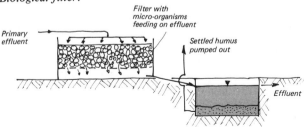

(b) Anaerobic up-flow filter in septic tank.

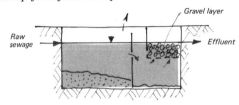

(c) Sand filter.

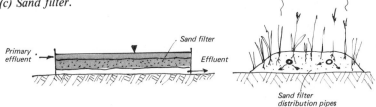

(d) Waste stabilization ponds.

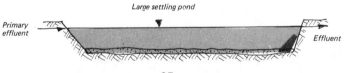

suitable for small domestic scale installations. Improvements are being made to sand filter systems to remove nitrates and phosphates from the effluent which can contaminate ground water used for drinking purposes; this may be necessary where on-site waste disposal systems are widely used on a regional basis.

Waste stabilization ponds provide a cheap and simple method of secondary treatment, especially in tropical countries where the temperature and sunlight encourage prolific growths of micro organisms (Figure 6d). The ponds allow mixed populations of bacteria and algae to feed on the organic matter in the effluent. Ponds are only suitable for the larger scale installations where they can be adequately maintained and protected from animals and children. They are also well described in the literature.

(d) Treatment processes in the soil

The soil soakaway allows tank effluent to be finally disposed of. The effluent is therefore out of sight and out of mind — that is, until the soakaway fails or groundwater levels rise carrying the effluent to the surface. The effluent adds to the natural liquid load on the soil which infiltrates through the soil surface, percolates between the soil particles, to drain away eventually to rivers and the sea through surface springs, or be evapo-transpired by surface vegetation.

Although the processes of infiltration and percolation into the soil look simple enough they are in fact difficult to measure, and scientists cannot predict with any accuracy how well a soil will accept water and how it will drain by examining its physical properties. The addition of an effluent containing dissolved and suspended solids makes the picture even more complex, as a crust is left at the soil face and the nutrients feed micro-organisms living in the soil pores causing them to become blocked. These processes will be described, however, in order to show how soakaway design can be approached in a rational manner.

Natural hydrology. The soil soakaway area chosen will already be receiving water from rain or snow, surface run-off from other less permeable ground or flooding from water courses. The amount of water being received will depend on the climate and geography; and its local intensity on the season and type of rain storm. During exceptionally heavy rainfall even the most permeable soil, unable to absorb all the water, may flood.

The nature of the soil surface largely determines the amount of rain water that infiltrates or runs off. Vegetation with its organic debris keeps the surface loose and open and slows down surface run-off; in contrast the pores of a bare soil may become clogged by the impact of the rain, reducing infiltration substantially. A flat, rough surface allows the water time to pond and soak in, but a smooth steep surface causes rapid runoff with little infiltration (see Figure 7a).

Once through the surface the rate at which the infiltrated water can percolate depends on the size of the pores between soil particles and their interconnectedness. Coarse-grained sandy soils are very permeable and make good soakaway beds; fine silts and clay soils, even though they may be relatively porous, have small pores with narrow connections and they are therefore impermeable. Fine grained soils can, however, hold a high moisture content through capillary action even when freely drained which may then be lost to the atmosphere by evapotranspiration through plants.

The larger scale structure of the soil also affects its permeability. Shrinkage cracks, root passages, and worm holes may make even a clay soil permeable enough for use as a soakaway. On the other hand, a thin clay layer near the surface of the coarsest sandy soil may effectively prevent adequate drainage (see Figure 7b).

The nature and characteristics of the surface soil, a complex science outside of the scope of this publication, depend on the materials making up the soil and the recent physical, chemical and bio-chemical processes involved in the soil's formation — influenced by factors such as rainfall, temperature, plant life, and soil organisms. Soils may vary in characteristics quite widely over even short distances. Depending on ground slope and the geomorphology of the area the permeability of a soil may be many times greater in a horizontal direction, due to sideways drainage of ground

Figure 7. Natural hydrology of soil infiltration and percolation.

(a) Infiltration through surface.

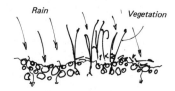

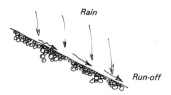

Loose, open surface, low slope.
Plants and plant debris

GOOD

Smooth, sealed surface
high slope

POOR

(b) Percolation through soil mass.

Large pores, interconnected cracks in
soil structure, root channels, worm holes

GOOD

Compacted soil, small pores with no
interconnection, generally clayey

POOR

(c) Ground water movement.

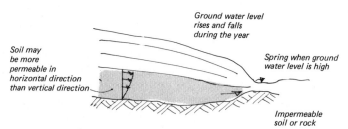

Ground water level
rises and falls
during the year

Soil may
be more
permeable in
horizontal direction
than vertical direction

Spring when ground
water level is high

Impermeable
soil or rock

water, than in a vertical direction (see Figure 7c). Soils in areas of heavy rainfall or with rapid groundwater movement are likely to be leached and permeable, making good soakaways.

The level of the groundwater table itself in the soakaway area is determined, for a given pattern of infiltrated rainfall, by the larger soil and geological structure. For isolated soakaways, however, the volume of effluent to be disposed of is small when compared to the volume of ground water from natural sources and the larger geological structure may usually be safely ignored. For large numbers of soakaways in a small area, or where large volumes of effluent are discharged into a small mass of soil, the geological structure must be investigated (Figure 7c).

Effluent disposal adds to the water from natural sources and puts a heavy liquid load onto the total soil body. The effluent does not have constant strength or flow but comes in surges as wastes are flushed through the systems; for poorly maintained tanks the quality of the effluent may sometimes be worse than that of the influent, as settled and digesting sewage is washed out. The effluent carries suspended solids and dissolved organic and inorganic materials.

The coarse solids are strained out at the soil surface zone and provide a filter which then traps even the finer sewage solids. This filter or crust provides a home for the growth of anaerobic micro-organisms which feed both on the crust and on the dissolved nutrients in the effluent (Figure 8a). This crust slows down the rate of infiltration and may lead to the eventual failure of the soakaway and to surface ponding, thus causing a potential health hazard. There is some evidence that the crust reduces infiltration to a very low rate which is maintainable over the long term. Experience suggests that resting the soakaway allows the crust to be degraded by aerobic micro-organisms and opened up by larger forms of soil life, such as worms; a longer period of resting allows a greater recovery in the permeability of the crust. The sand filters described above in effect allow this crust to be scraped off and removed.

The dissolved organic materials that infiltrate with the

effluent through the crust are, in turn, used as nutrients and are mineralized by micro-organisms living in the soil mass itself. The dissolved inorganics or salts may cause a swelling of some clay particles reducing permeability — or the effluent may improve permeability by leaching out salts that already existed in the soil. The potential effects of dissolved salts on the soil can be determined by chemical tests, but these are not usually carried out for isolated soakaways or where clay content is low. In areas where large numbers of dwellings dispose of water-borne effluent through soakaways the dissolved salts can seriously contaminate the groundwater. This is a serious problem where the groundwater is an essential source of drinking water and in these circumstances the effluent must be either further treated before disposal into the soil, or disposed of in other ways.

Perhaps more dangerous to health than salts in groundwater is the travel of pathogens, or disease-causing micro-organisms, through the soil from the effluent. The survival of the pathogens depends on the species, the nutrient levels, the presence or absence of oxygen, pH, moisture content, temperature, competition from the soil's micro-organisms and soil porosity; most pathogens find the soil an alien environment and die off quickly but others may survive for long periods. A high proportion of the pathogens are removed by the soil crust and others are adsorbed onto the surface of soil particles and die off. The distance that the pathogens may travel and remain viable depends on the ability of the crust zone and soil to remove then, and the proximity and velocity of flow of the groundwater (see Figure 8b). In a coarse sandy soil the pathogens may travel long distances and be present in the groundwater taken from wells, bore-holes or springs. In fine-grained, unsaturated soils where crusting has been established the pathogens may be considered to be removed within one metre of the soakaway. No firm rules governing the removal of pathogens can be made for soakaway systems, however, and it should always be assumed that there is some risk of groundwater contamination until proved otherwise.

Figure 8. Effect of effluent on soakaway.

(a) Clogging of soakaway.

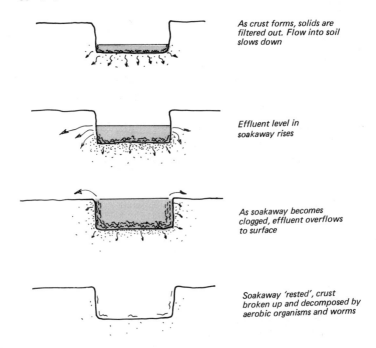

As crust forms, solids are filtered out. Flow into soil slows down

Effluent level in soakaway rises

As soakaway becomes clogged, effluent overflows to surface

Soakaway 'rested', crust broken up and decomposed by aerobic organisms and worms

(b) High water table can become contaminated by pathogens.

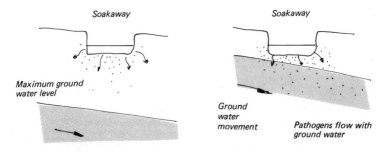

Soakaway

Soakaway

Maximum ground water level

Ground water movement

Pathogens flow with ground water

33

3 DESIGN OF THE SETTLING TANK

The settling tank of aqua-privy and septic tank systems provides conditions in which the solids in the sewage may settle, consolidate and be partially digested. The complex nature of the treatment processes has already been outlined; tank design has to take into account widely varying conditions:

Quantity of sewage to be treated and time of discharge depends on
—water supply availability, whether piped to house or carried from a standpipe
—continuity of water supply through day
—number of people using the system
—amount of sullage, or washing water, discharged to the tank

Solids in sewage to settle and form sludge depend on
—diet of users
—material used for anal cleaning
—type of sullage, if included

Processes in tank depend on
—retention time of liquor, affecting the settlement of solids
—frequency of removal of sludge and scum
—temperature of tank contents, average and minimum
—surges from incoming sewage.

Minimum recommended tank sizes for different populations are shown in Figure 9; these have been developed from experience in the different countries and indicate the great variation in design parameters and approaches to design.

A more rigorous approach to design estimates the sludge build-up in the bottom of the tank between desludging from the solids load in the incoming sewage, allows for digestion over the period, and gives a tank size that still allows adequate retention time in the supernatant layer for efficient solids settling, or even with the sludge and scum build-up. A general expression for tank size is given as:

34

Where

Tank design capacity = capacity needed for sludge and scum storage between desludging (A)
+ capacity needed for sewage retention and settling in the supernatant layer just before desludging. (B)

or $C = P \times n \times f \times s + P \times r \times q$

C = tank capacity (litres)

P = number of people using the system

n = number of years between desludging — this is often assumed to be three years, but in practice, tanks should be desludged more often than this — say twice a year

f = factor relating rate of sludge digestion to temperature; at low temperatures digestion is slow and extra capacity is needed

s = rate of sludge and scum accumulation after active digestion; this depends on materials used for anal cleansing as well as the volume of waste water received by the tank

r = minimum retention time required in tank for solids settlement, often taken to be 1 day

q = sewage flow generated for each person using the tank (litres/person/day).

The minimum tank size should be $C = 1.5 \times Pnfs$. Examples of calculations to determine tank capacity are given in Figure 10. A larger tank size than that calculated will give extra storage volume for sludge and extra retention time improving settlement.

Tank dimensions are chosen to give the minimum liquid capacity calculated, but they will also depend on other aspects such as ease of construction and maintenance, or use of standard size components in construction. The minimum tank width is usually taken to be 600mm, if a man has to enter it before or after construction; for an aqua-privy the plan area of the tank must be large enough to accommodate both the squatting slab and removable cover for desludging.

A rectangular plan shape is often recommended for septic tanks with length three times the width (Figure 11). The tank is divided up into two compartments to help reduce turbulence caused by inflow, the first with a length twice that of the second. These compartments are separated by a baffle and the liquor flows into the second compartment through horizontal slots which must be below the scum layer. The depth of liquid may be between 1.2 and 1.5m, the latter being more usual; there should be a clearance of at least 300mm between water level and roof. For aqua-privies the depth may be about 1.0m and the capacity *(C)* is usually between 1,000 and 1,800 litres. The tank capacity given by these recommended minimum dimensions must be checked against calculated minimum capacity, and the minimum capacity required by local regulations.

Figure 9. Minimum recommended tank sizes (WEDC, 1979).

Code of practice	Population	Minimum Capacities (m^3 or 10^3litre) where Desludging Period is		
		6 months	one year	two years
Part I	5	—	1.12	1.18
	10	—	1.80	2.52
	15	—	2.34	3.60
	20	2.53	3.30	4.55
	50	5.60	7.28	10.04
Part II	100	—	22.40	23.30
	150	—	28.60	32.90
	200	—	38.40	44.20
	300	—	56.90	65.50

Note: minimum capacity = 1 m^3

Tanks of many different shapes and configurations have been constructed and operated successfully. The rectangular shape is well suited to the bricks and blocks traditionally used in construction and is widely described in the technical literature of many countries.

Figure 10. Examples of tank sizing (Pickford, 1980).

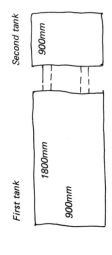

Figure 10a. Plan and dimensions, Example 1.

Example 1. Septic tank: climate cold in winter: house with full plumbing: continuous water supply: all waste water to tank: sludge removal every three years.

First stage:

A = Pnfs

Temperature less than 10°C in winter, n = 3, so f = 1.27

Soft paper used for anal cleaning, sullage to tank, so S = 40 l/pa

Therefore A = $6 \times 3 \times 1.27 \times 40$ = 912 litres

Second stage:

B = Pq

Full water connections, so q = 120 l/pd

B = 6×120 = 720 litres

B = 6×200 = 1,200 litres

Total capacity:

B is more than half A, so

C = A + B = 912 + 720 = 1,632 litres

1632 litres = 1.632 cubic metres

With a depth of 1.5 metres, the plan area of the tank is 1.088 cubic metres. With two compartments, the areal dimensions of Figure 10a would be suitable.

Figure 10b. Plan and dimensions, Example 2.

Example 2. Septic tank: temperature during year 15°C-30°C: house with full plumbing and luxurious use of water: all waste water to tank: sludge removal every ten years.

First stage:

A = Pnfs

Temperature more than 10°C throughout the year, n = 10, so f = 1.0

Soft paper for anal cleaning, sullage to tank, so s = 40 l/pa

Therefore A = $6 \times 10 \times 40$ = 2,400 litres

Second stage:

B = Pq

Luxurious use of water, so q = 200 l/pd

B = 6×200 = 1,200 litres

Total capacity:

B is equal to half A, so C = A + B = 3,600 litres

3600 litres = 3.6 cubic metres

With a depth of 1.5 metres, the plan area is 2.4 square metres

With two compartments, a suitable size would be as shown in Figure 10b.

Inlet and outlet pipes must allow the tank influent and effluent to flow freely without becoming blocked by the developing scum layer or disturbing the settled sludge. The inlet pipe must introduce the raw sewage in a way that does not cause short-circuiting in the tank.

For single household septic tanks the most common inlet device is a 'T' shaped junction that deflects the incoming sewage downwards and allows the bend to be rodded, if blocked, from above (Figure 12a). The inlet pipe level is set 25mm above liquid level in the tank to be free-draining to prevent backing up and blockage of the inlet pipe, and allow the tank and pipe to be ventilated.

In larger installations serving schools or hospitals the inlet may consist of two bends fed from an inspection chamber, with a baffle plate across the width of the tank to deflect flow downwards.

Surge flows into the tank from flushing WCs, unplugged baths or sinks, may be reduced by laying the last 12 metres or more of the inlet pipe to a gradient not greater than 2 per cent (1 in 50), and having a diameter of at least 100mm.

Figure 11. Basic septic tank dimensions.

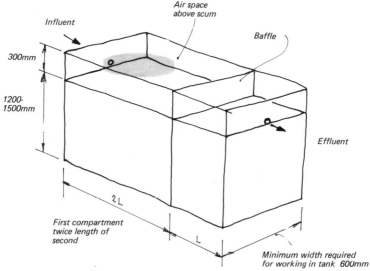

38

Figure 12. Tank sections.

(a) Inlet and outlet pipes.

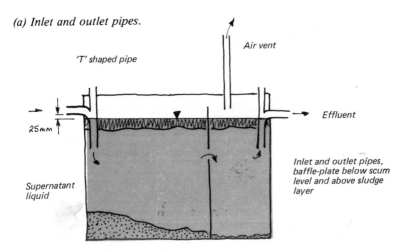

'T' shaped pipe

Air vent

Effluent

25mm

Supernatant
liquid

Inlet and outlet pipes,
baffle-plate below scum
level and above sludge
layer

(b) Aqua-privy down pipe.

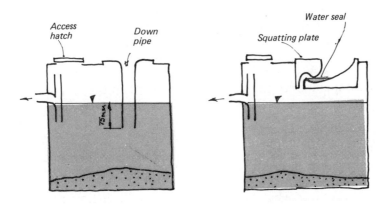

Access
hatch

Down
pipe

Water seal

Squatting plate

75mm

Aqua-privies are usually fitted with a squatting slab and chute formed by a vertical pipe which extends at least 75mm below liquid level; if these are made from glass smooth materials the risks of sticking faeces and fouling will be reduced — a sloping down-pipe will also assist efficient flushing, (Figure 12b). Alternatively the aqua-privy may be fitted with a simple water seal.

Outlets for both aqua-privies and small septic tanks are also made from a simple T-shaped junction with a down-pipe extending below the scum layer into the supernatant liquor. The level of the outlet pipe determines the water level in the tank (Figure 12a, b).

For larger septic tank installations a baffle plate extending across the tank width holds the scum away from an overflow weir. This arrangement reduces strong localized currents in the supernatant liquor and reduces the risks of short-circuiting or drawing up settled sludge.

Ventilation is needed to allow the gases from the digesting sludge to escape. These consist mostly of carbon dioxide and methane, but will also contain small amounts of other gases, many of them foul smelling. For septic tank systems the gases may be ventilated through the inlet pipe and out of a screened stack pipe near the top of the sewer. Local regulations may demand an air valve on the tank itself (Figure 12a).

For aqua-privies the gases can be vented from a stack pipe fitted to the tank itself (See Figure 1). Experience has shown that if the systems are operating well, and a scum layer has been built up, the tanks will smell musty and 'sweet'. Foul and obnoxious odours arise when the methanogenic bacteria do not metabolize the volatile acids — when they have been destroyed by toxins or acid conditions, for instance.

4 DESIGN OF THE SOIL SOAKAWAY

As already explained, it is not possible to predict with any accuracy what the effect of the effluent will be on the soakaway, nor what the safe, long term dosing rate should be. The difficulty researchers have found in understanding the complex processes involved in soil soakaways excavation has led to a confusing diversity of approaches in design:

(i) Some suggest that the soakaway base becomes blocked with settled solids and that most infiltration takes place mainly through the sides, despite their small surface area. Others point out that the shallow depth of effluent leads to unsaturated conditions in the soil at the sides with most infiltration taking place through the base, even though it may be partially clogged.

(ii) These arguments call for soakaway trenches that are either deep and narrow to increase side wall area, or wide and shallow to increase base area; a combination of these has been proposed — a deep narrow trench below the drain and a wide trench at drain level.

(iii) Dosing is recommended to be intermittent, but some tests have shown that continuous dosing increases the volumes of effluent that can be infiltrated per unit time.

(iv) Resting the soakaway to permit aerobic decomposition of the crust, and its break-up by worms, is said to improve the infiltration rate, but others consider this to be a harmful or an unnecessary practice.

(v) Some soakaways are designed to distribute the effluent over a number of parallel trenches, whereas other take it along one continuous trench with the first section being the most heavily loaded.

In practice the flow of effluent is not constant and the trench will be alternately flooded and drained, exposing the crust to periodic aerobic decomposition.

Temperature, rainfall, soil type and profile, soil micro-organisms, will also affect the soakaway behaviour; the effects these factors have in causing variation in soakaway behaviour will be compounded by the pattern of effluent flow and strength that may be expected at different times and places. Most research on soakaway systems has been carried out in North America where soakaways have failed and flooded during cold, wet winter months under high effluent discharges; very little work has been carried out in hot, dry climates.

Soil and site investigations will, nevertheless, give some idea of the suitability of an area for a soil soakaway. On some sites a failed soakaway can be replaced by a second soakaway

41

relatively cheaply and inadequate design will not be disastrous. It is on small crowded sites that adequate sizing becomes essential and where failure can lead to serious health hazards. Soil investigations look at the more local behaviour of the soil directly adjacent to the soakaway system; site investigations examine the larger environmental conditions and earth mass containing the soakaway (Table 5). Each of these investigations is a separate field of study in itself and they are described only briefly below.

(a) Site characteristics and environment

Climate. Soils which experience regular heavy rainfall and can absorb storms without surface flooding are likely to be leached and permeable. Dry soils in hot climates that have a caked surface and have low infiltration rates may still be satisfactory as a soakaway once the surface layer is removed.

Higher temperatures reduce the viscosity of water and allow it to flow more easily through soil pores; at high temperatures the micro-organisms are most active in decomposing the solids in the effluent and in feeding on the nutrients. Lower temperatures have the reverse effects. Frozen ground obviously cannot accept effluent.

Topography and geology. A brief site inspection will indicate the likely drainage patterns of the area. Sites on higher ground, or on relatively steep slopes are likely to be well drained; soakaway sites under banks may be flooded by surface run off from uphill or have groundwater close to the surface. Local ditches may cause flooding, or drain the effluent percolating through the soil; nearby wet ground indicates poor local drainage. Well established trees have a root system that generally opens up the soil structure. Rock outcrops nearby should be carefully examined as they may form an impermeable base to the soakaway area preventing the movement of groundwater.

This aspect of site investigation should use local knowledge and records, and an inspection should be made of such potential problems as road or drain cuttings, or wells.

Population. Septic tanks handling large volumes of waste

cannot be used with soil soakaway systems on crowded sites because there will not be adequate area for the drainage trenches; therefore secondary treatment and other precautions are necessary if the tanks must be used (Figure 3); aqua-privies need small soakaways and are sometimes more suitable for crowded areas. The prime purpose of the soakaway is to isolate and dispose of the pathogen-ridden effluent below ground level; failure of the soakaway will cause surface flooding and become a health hazard. The soakaway site should, if possible, be fenced off — or at least isolated from children or animals.

Groundwater movement. The relatively small amounts of effluent will not affect the pattern of groundwater movement significantly, but seasonal changes in groundwater level may cause the soakaway to flood to the surface if the water level rises too high. Some indication of groundwater movement may be found from local records and observation — the emergence of springs during wet periods, for instance. Groundwater movement will often remain an unknown factor.

The removal of pathogens in the soil is not certain and soakaways should be placed as far as possible from wells or springs used for drinking purposes; some authorities recommend a minimum distance of at least 30 metres. Surface flooding from high groundwater levels can result in effluent being washed into nearby streams causing contamination.

(b) Soil characteristics

Soil texture often indicates the likely permeability of a soil, coarse-grained sandy soils being more permeable than clay and loam soils. It has been suggested that general maximum loading rates for various soils should be based on the following:

Sands and silty loams	50 mm/day
Sandy loams (where pores are blocked with fine silt)	30 mm/day
Clay soils	10 mm/day

Table 5. Evaluating the site of a soil soakaway.

Site characteristics and environment		Soil characteristics	
Climate	— Rainfall distribution through the year, and storm intensities that cause local surface run-off. — Temperature and possibility of snow or frozen ground.	*Soil texture* *Soil colour* *Soil structure* *Soil profiles* *Soil tests*	grain size and composition indicating good or bad drainage affects permeability soil layers below soakaway
Topography and geology	— Position of site in relation to higher and lower ground; slope of site. — Proximity to ditches, or stream beds. — Proximity to wet ground. — Nature of land surface; vegetation. — Geological structure of area.	Crust test Chemical test Percolation test	ability of soil to draw water by capillary action through crust effect of effluent salts on clay fraction in soil permeability of soil
Population	— Size of site and proximity to dwellings; present use of site.		
Groundwater movement	— Groundwater movement in soil and drainage. — Rise and fall of groundwater through year. — Use of groundwater for drinking purposes; distance of soakaway from water source.		

44

These are very approximate values that have been used in North America. With practice the composition of a sample of soil can be estimated reasonably well by spreading it out in the palm of the hand; clay soils are plastic when moist and easily identified.

Soil colour. Well drained subsoils have a brown, red or yellowish brown colour with little mottling. Poorly drained subsoils are mottled or multi-coloured grey and are too wet for the infiltration of effluents.

Soil structure may have a significant influence upon percolation rates. Blocky, prismatic and columnar structures are associated with soils suitable for soakaway systems; compact, dense soils are likely to be impermeable. Soil structure can be examined in the walls of an excavated trench, which will also reveal root channels and shrinkage cracks.

Soil profiles show the nature of the subsoil and any local impermeable layers that may underlie the site.

SOIL TESTS

Crust test. This test estimates the strength of capillary action in the soil. It measures the rate at which water is drawn through a filter by a partially saturated soil; it is an attempt to model the effect of a surface crust in the soakaway system. The crust test requires sophisticated equipment and is not often used.

Chemical tests try and establish the soils' sensitivity to salts — that is, whether or not the salts will cause the clay portion to swell and to block up the soil pores. This test also requires laboratory equipment to carry out.

Percolation tests are described in most of the design handbooks and standards on soil soakaway systems. They assume that the rate at which a soil will accept effluent over the long term is related to the rate at which it can initially absorb tap water. This assumption is clearly too optimistic, as it ignores the solids load of the effluent.

The standard percolation test procedure given in the American *Manual of Septic Tank Practice* (USDHEW, 1959) is as follows:

> Six or more separate 100-300 mm diameter test holes, spaced uniformly over the proposed absorption field site, are dug or bored to the depth of the base of the proposed seepage bed. The sides and bottom of each hole are then scratched to restore a natural soil interface. Loose material is removed from the hole and a 50 mm layer of coarse sand or fine gravel is spread on the bottom.

> To conduct the test the hole is filled to a depth of 300 mm with clean water. This depth of water is maintained for at least four hours — and preferably overnight — to saturate the soil and develop such particle swelling as may be characteristic of the soil. The percolation rate is then determined 24 hours after first wetting of the hole, the procedure depending on whether or not water remains in the hole overnight.

Figure 13. Estimation of soakage area required.

Example

Effluent to be disposed of $\quad= Q$ litres/day

Depth soaking in 30 mins $\quad= d$ metres

Volume soaking in 30 mins/m² $= d \times 10^3$ litres

Volume soaking in 24 hours/m² $= d \times 48 \times 10^3$ litres

Soakage area required $\quad= \dfrac{d \times 48 \times 10^3}{Q}$ m²,

(This area should be checked with areas used locally or with area delivered from CP302, 1972).

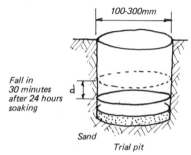

Trial pit

If the hole contains water the depth is brought up to 150 mm and the fall in water level measured over a 30 minute period. If no water remains in the hole overnight, the level is maintained at a 150 mm depth for four hours, topping up as necessary. The drop that occurs in the final 30 minute period is then used to determine the bottom area required in trenches or seepage beds, or the wall area of seepage pits. For sandy soils the interval of observation is reduced from 30 to 10 minutes.

Figure 14. Seepage pits.

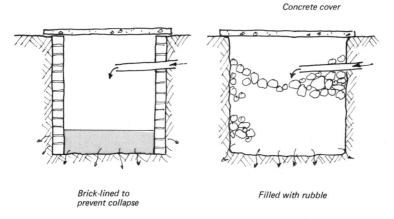

Concrete cover

Brick-lined to prevent collapse

Filled with rubble

(c) Design loading rates

Percolation tests give only a very rough indication of the long term behaviour of a soakaway system disposing of effluent. They give no indication of the effect of effluent salts on the soil, or clogging the solids, or microbial growth blocking soil pores. Until there is more solid evidence relating to the values found in these tests to actual field experience it is recommended that the more conservative values from CP 302, (1972) *Small sewage treatment works* are used in trench or pit design using the following relationship:

$$q = \frac{360}{t}$$ where q = design loading (litres/day/m²)
t = percolation test rate (seconds/mm)

47

The length of trench, or bottom area of seepage pit needed, may then be estimated knowing population and volume of effluent per day (see Figure 13).

(d) System layout and construction

Seepage pits are appropriate for small septic tank systems built in areas with very permeable soil, or for aqua-privy systems with their small volumes of effluent. The seepage pit is simply a covered hole excavated into the ground, supported internally by a porous lining of brick work or by back-filled stones (Figure 14). They are cheap to make, and use only a small area.

The pit may be up to 5m deep and up to 2.5m in diameter, but for aqua-privy systems can be very much smaller — perhaps an equivalent volume to the tank itself. The soil surface of the pit may be expected to block up in time and the pit will then have to be replaced, perhaps every 5-10 years. A simple replaceable filter installed at the top of a stone-filled pit will screen out the effluent solids and lengthen the life of the pit — the filter may be scraped clean and replaced at the same time as the tank is de-sludged.

Deep seepage pits should be chosen with care where there is a risk of penetrating and contaminating a groundwater body which is extracted nearby for drinking purposes. Some authorities suggest that the bottom of the pit should terminate at least 1.2m above the ground water table.

Brickwork for hole lining should be carefully laid and the space between the bricks and excavated soil backfilled with gravel or coarse sand to provide support. When loaded, the brick cylinder formed during construction is placed in compression: seepage gaps between the bricks are therefore best left between layers. If the bricks are carefully placed, mortar is not needed. Care must be taken during the construction of a deep pit that the sides do not collapse and smother the people digging it.

Soakage trenches have open jointed pipes, bedded in coarse gravel, that carry the effluent along the trench. The effluent leaks out of the pipes, seeps through the gravel and infiltrates into the soil (Figures 15a, b).

48

Several authorities recommend that a long continuous trench be used, but several shorter trenches fed from a distribution box to ensure equal pipe loading allow the soil to be more evenly loaded and provide facilities for resting the trenches in turn (Figure 15c). The effluent load will vary through the day and the trenches will be alternatively soaked and drained. Distribution boxes are also used where the soakaway area has a steep slope. However, in a well graded trench low spots will be more heavily loaded and will tend to clog up first.

The soil surfaces of the excavated trench should not become smeared, compacted or silted up during construction as this reduces the rate of infiltration that can be achieved even before the crust has formed. Smearing blocks up the surface pores and occurs when the soil is cut or trimmed by a spade; the soil surfaces should be brushed and scarified before the gravel is placed. Compaction is caused by the diggers walking up and down in the excavated trench, especially when the soil is damp. Rain flooding the open trench during construction will wash silt or clay into the surface pores; if flooding occurs the surface layers should be raked out and removed.

The trenches should have a gradient not exceeding 1 in 200 to prevent the rapid flow of effluent along the trench and possible surface ponding at the downhill end. They are excavated with widths from 300-1,000mm and have a 150mm gravel layer in the base. This gravel is generally recommended to be from 20-50mm in size, with large open pores that allow the effluent to flow across the full width of the trench. Fine gravel is sometimes used that acts both as a filter and bacteria bed. Unglazed clay tile drains butted end to end are suitable for carrying the effluent along the trench, but any pipe that is porous, of reasonable strength, durable and cheap may be used. These are laid on the bottom layer of gravel and the trenches are backfilled with gravel to the crown of the pipes (see Figure 15a).

After the gravel backfill and drains have been installed they are covered with a thick layer of hay, straw, leaves, turf or hessian to prevent the backfilled soil from being washed down and blocking the gravel layer. Soil from the original

Figure 15. Design of soakage trench.

(a) Cross-section.

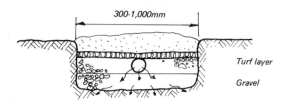

(b) Longitudinal section.

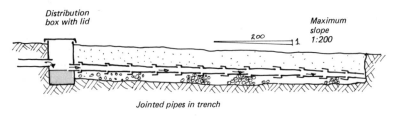

(c) Plan.

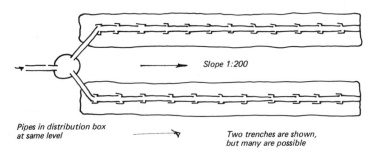

excavation is then backfilled into the trench and left mounded at the surface to allow for settlement (see Figure 15a). The gravel cover and soil still allow air to reach the trench base during periods between dosing. The earth cover should be deep enough to protect the drain pipes from damage but should be above groundwater level.

A grass cover over the trench helps bind the surface and backfill, and take some of the effluent in evapotranspiration. Larger plants, shrubs and trees are not to be grown above the pipes in case the roots penetrate and block them.

It must be emphasized that an optimum method of designing and operating soakaway systems is not known; and little experimental work has been carried out on the behaviour of soil soakways under tropical conditions.

5 OPERATION AND MAINTENANCE

A newly-built septic tank or aqua-privy should be tested for water-tightness by filling it with water and allowing the water to stand for a day. The water need not be piped drinking water if there is a stream, well or irrigation canal nearby. After testing, the tank should be left full of water. The commencement of digestion is helped by throwing in some sludge from an old tank.

The only maintenance necessary for well-constructed and properly-used septic tanks and aqua-privies is the removal of surplus sludge and scum to leave a clear central zone for settlement. Proper use of an aqua-privy involves keeping the squatting plate clean and ensuring that the drop pipe in the tank does not stand clear of the water level, by adding enough water to make up for evaporation or leakage. If the chute becomes blocked it may be necessary to clear it with a stick.

Regular inspection of the tank is necessary to find out whether the sludge and scum levels are acceptable — a septic tank should be inspected at half the design sludging interval. If hard indigestible material is used for anal cleansing the sludge level in a small aqua-privy should be checked more frequently.

The most satisfactory method of sludge removal is to use a tanker lorry equipped with a sludge pump and flexible suction hose. Removable covers should be provided for all compartments of septic tanks and are best at the inlet ends where sludge accumulation is greatest. If the suction pipe is lowered down the chute of an aqua-privy damage often results to the chute. Therefore a removable access cover should be built in the top or side of the tank.

The bottom of the sludge layer is usually well-consolidated and a high proportion of the material may be cemented together by fine particles. Most of this material should be removed. Some tanker lorries are equipped with a hosepipe so that a jet of water can stir up the hard deposits. If a jet is not available the sludge should be disturbed with the end of the suction pipe or with a stick or long-handled spade.

When a tanker lorry is not available, it is usual to dig out the sludge with a long-handled shovel, and to remove it in buckets or tins. This is unpleasant work and can be a health hazard, as the sludge will still contain some pathogenic micro-organisms. A cheap alternative used in some places is an animal-drawn tank fitted with a hand-operated suction pipe.

By whatever means it is collected, the material removed from the tank is a mixture of harmless matter (such as sand and well digested sludge) and potentially harmful fresh sewage and undigested sludge. It can only safely be used for agriculture or horticulture when persistent pathogens have been eliminated — for example by a long period of drying or by composting with vegetable waste. The provision of a sound collection and disposal service is essential for the health of the community.

A septic tank should never be completely emptied. Some old sludge should always be left at the bottom to ensure that digestion continues, a practice known as 'seeding'. It is particularly important to fill the tank of an aqua-privy quickly after desludging so that the bottom of the downpipe is covered.

One of the obvious causes for the failure of septic tank or aqua-privy systems is the filling of the tank with sludge, which restricts space for settling of solids. These then flow straight into the soakaway and quickly clog up the soil.

CHAPTER THREE

Construction Details of a Ferrocement Septic Tank Designed for the U.K. Market

This chapter gives construction details and materials specifications for a ferrocement septic tank designed for use in the rural areas of Britain. There are about one million people in these areas, where waterborne sewerage is prohibitively expensive, who use a variety of on-site waste disposal systems. The most common option now in use is the septic tank and ground soakaway, an installation which is grant-aided by local authorities, needs planning permission before it is built, and is rigorously inspected both during and after construction.

In Britain the design and specification for septic tanks is covered by CP302:1972 — *Small Sewage Treatment Works* which recommends dimensions, pipe-work arrangement and materials for a two-chamber rectangular tank. The products of the prefabricated septic tank market have to conform to this code and/or be field-tested to the satisfaction of an examining authority.

The septic tank described below, developed in Gwynedd, North Wales, had therefore to fulfil the following conditions. It must:

satisfy recommendations of CP302:1972 and all other official regulations,

be of comparable cost with alternative products,

offer distinct advantages in terms of handling and installation,

be durable and simple to maintain.

Figure 16. Septic tank designs.

(a) In situ brick/block tanks.

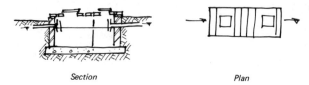

Section   Plan

(b) Pre-fabricated tanks.

Pre-cast re-inforced concrete rings
with joints mortared water tight

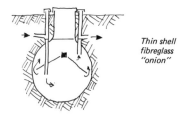

R.C. rings with joints mortared water tight.

Section   Plan

(c) Fibreglass onion.

Thin shell
fibreglass
"onion"

(d) Pre-cast concrete panels.

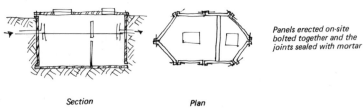

Panels erected on-site
bolted together and the
joints sealed with mortar

Section   Plan

54

1 ALTERNATIVES AVAILABLE

(a) In situ tanks

These are built from bricks or blocks — mortar rendered on the inside to make them watertight — constructed on a mass concrete base poured in the bottom of the excavation. The tanks are either covered over with a reinforced concrete slab (Figure 16a) or with concrete or timber planks. These tanks are perfectly satisfactory, being simple to de-sludge through manholes cast in the roof. They take a long time to construct, however, and there is a risk of the excavation collapsing or flooding in wet climates during the building works.

(b) Pre-fabricated tanks

These can be installed and the excavation backfilled in the same day, if a suitable digging machine is available, and are made from a variety of materials. The most common are described below.

Pre-cast reinforced concrete rings used for large diameter drains and manholes have been widely adapted for septic tank construction. Two columns of rings are used to form two chambers with a pipe connection between them to carry the settled sewage (Figure 16b). The rings are built up on a concrete base cast at the base of the excavation. The joint between the rings is sealed with shaped strips of rubber, or the entire inside face of the rings is mortar-rendered to prevent leaks. The rings are generally too heavy to be manhandled and a machine is used to lower them, especially the commercial 'spun' pipes. Tanks made in this way are very durable and can take exceptional traffic loads without cracking; they are accessible to easy de-sludging, but soil settling in poorly compacted fill can fracture the connecting pipe. Difficulties are often experienced if holes for the inlet and outlet pipes are not cast into the concrete and have to be cut out on site.

Fibreglass septic tanks have rapidly become popular in Britain and at least four manufacturers are supplying the distinctive 'onion' or bottle design with a range of sizes

(Figure 16c). This design withstands soil loads through its spheroidal shape braced internally by baffles which also form the division between compartments. The tanks are light enough to be manhandled into the most difficult locations without a machine; if ground water is expected the tanks have to be weighted with a ring of concrete around the neck. The fibreglass shell is either laid onto moulds by hand or sprayed by machine during construction. The shell is very thin and is easily punctured by stones and the backfill has to be carefully selected and placed. Fibreglass resists corrosion from sewage. The bottle shape only allows access for de-sludging using a suction pump. Blockages cannot be cleared by hand — which may cause difficulties where non-biodegradable solid objects are used for anal cleansing. Fibreglass tanks of this sort are being exported and used in several developing countries.

Ferrocement tanks have been used extensively in New Zealand for many years. They are built in one piece, including partitions, and do not need rendering inside after construction for sealing against leakages. The tanks are too heavy to manhandle and a machine or tackle is required to lower them into the excavation. They are very strong and do not need selected backfill to prevent puncturing by stones. Their weight, in comparison with the fibreglass tanks, has an advantage that uplift in wet ground is prevented — which sometimes occurs when the fibreglass tanks are de-sludged.

Pre-cast concrete panels can be carried to the site, erected quickly by hand, and bolted together to form a tank (Figure 16d). The panels are cast in a concrete yard using accurate moulds which must be carefully maintained to ensure that the bolt holes line up accurately. For small tanks the panels need only nominal reinforcement. After construction, the tank is finished and sealed inside with a layer of mortar to prevent leaks. Tanks made in this way have great advantage in congested or inaccessible areas where haulage vehicles, excavating plant or lifting tackle is not available or cannot reach the installation site easily, and in Calcutta, are often built on the ground surface, not in an excavation.

Figure 17. Aqua-privy constructed from pre-fabricated reinforced concrete panels.

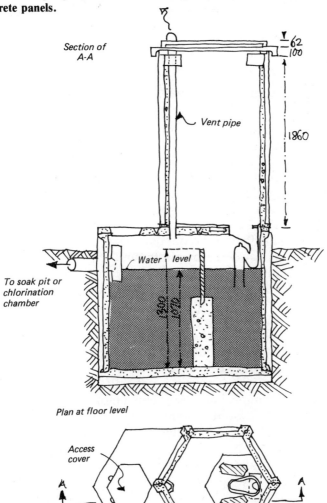

Section of A-A

62
100

Vent pipe

1860

Water level

To soak pit or chlorination chamber

Plan at floor level

Access cover

A

A

Door

Over 30,000 of these have been installed in the bustee areas of Calcutta (dimensions in millimetres).

Other materials such as steel plate have also been used for pre-fabricated tanks but these are expensive to construct and difficult to protect against corrosion.

2 FERROCEMENT SEPTIC TANK DESIGN

(a) Ferrocement — its properties

Ferrocement is a thin shell structural material made by hand-plastering a cement-rich mortar into several layers of wire mesh fabric. Cement mortar shrinks as it sets and the mesh distributes the shrinkage cracks in the curing mortar. It also distributes applied loads through the layer — in this way the tensile strength of the mortar is fully developed before tensile or bending failure occurs through definite fracture planes.

The mesh and wire reinforcement in ferrocement shells are conventionally laid up before plastering; in the design shown in Figure 18, however, the plaster and reinforcement are laid up at the same time in layers onto formwork which is stripped out after the mortar has set. In this way a thin dense shell can be made. Ferrocement shells do not have the air cavities that present a serious risk with conventional thin reinforced concrete shells poured between two shutters.

Ferrocement is strong and elastic, corrosion resistant, exceptionally durable — and well-proven in practice in many countries over many years. It is not a difficult material to use, needing only simple hand tools and a mortar mixer — mixing can also be carried out by hand; skills with the basic materials are commonly used in other building activities. A more complete description of the properties and advantages of ferrocement is given in Watt (1978).

Thin shell ferrocement structures achieve their exceptional strength through the designed curved surfaces, curves that are difficult to construct using conventional reinforced concrete.

(b) Tank design

The first design chosen was elliptical in plan with vertical walls, having an internal partition separating the tank into two chambers. The ellipsoid shape was chosen in order to utilize the strength of curved shells, and to reduce the possibility that the authorities would not approve of a design that differed too much from the recommendations of the Code of Practice.

Construction of the formwork for the ellipse was found to be difficult. Bending the plywood form face to the tight curves at the tank ends to make an accurate shape proved a particularly lengthy business. During the construction of the tank itself it was found even more difficult to bend the mesh and reinforcing wire around the tank ends tightly enough to give a thin shell; on the flat curves of the sides the mesh

Figure 18. Cylindrical ferrocement septic tank.

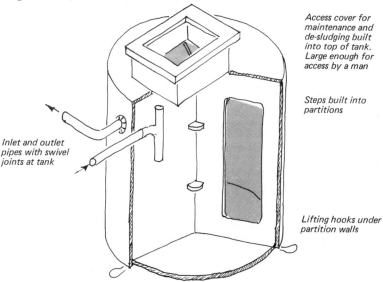

Access cover for maintenance and de-sludging built into top of tank. Large enough for access by a man

Steps built into partitions

Inlet and outlet pipes with swivel joints at tank

Lifting hooks under partition walls

Sectional view of tank showing first settlement zone.

Quantities (for tank of 3,200 l capacity)

Cement		300kg
Sand		700kg
Reinforcement	Galvanized weld mesh (walls)	16sq m
	— Ungalvanized weld mesh (flows, partitions)	12sq m
	Hoop wire	100m
Fillings	— Pipes, T bends, Swivel joint	
Poly-vinyl acetate (PVA)		

would not lie flat. It is essential that the position of the mesh be accurately controlled on the formwork, otherwise the shell thickness becomes overbuilt and too heavy.

This design was abandoned for one with a circular shape. These initial difficulties have been described in order to show that considerable developmental work is necessary on any prototype design before it reaches the manufacturing stage. They also demonstrate that attempting to anticipate the objections of the authorities should take second place to using the materials in a sound and efficient way.

The final tank design that evolved from experience, whose construction is described at length in this chapter, has a circular plan with three internal panels giving support to the walls. This design has proved simple and fool-proof to construct and install and is shown in Figure 18.

The curves, being sections of a circle, are simple to construct in ferrocement, and the formwork components are interchangeable with each other. The circular shape is exceptionally strong and allows the shell to develop high resistance to external soil loads and internal liquid pressures.

This tank design had to compete with both fibreglass and concrete ring tanks in Gwynedd, both in price and ease of installation. The inlet and outlet pipes were required to swivel to ease alignment during installation, and the cover had to be adjustable in height to suit the drain depth and depth of excavation. Quantities of materials used are also shown in Figure 12.

3 CONSTRUCTION SITE AND MATERIALS

(a) Yard layout

A major requirement of the construction yard is that the tanks should be built under cover from the sun, rain and wind. If the wet mortar is exposed to strong sunlight it dries too quickly leaving large shrinkage cracks that seriously weaken the shell and leave the wire reinforcement open to corrosion; overheating also occurs if the tank is built outside and covered closely with plastic sheeting which has a greenhouse effect. Rain washes the mortar off the formwork and strong winds can dry the mortar out prematurely. Ideally the cover should be watertight, be clad against prevailing winds, and high enough not to interfere with construction work or handling.

The layout of the yard should be planned to ease the handling of materials and tools. A concrete pad is needed on which the tanks can be constructed. A dry shed in which to store lockaway tools, equipment and formwork against theft is useful (Figure 19). The bags of cement should be stacked on raised wooden pallets and used in the same order they were purchased — damp cement forms lumps which weaken the tanks and make trowelling difficult.

The sand should also be protected especially from animals, children or debris; covering the sand against the weather helps keep the moisture content uniform. The mesh and wire may be stored in the open — slight oxidation or rusting of the surfaces allows them to bond more securely to the mortar. Ungalvanised mesh should not rust too much, however.

The mortar mixer, if it is powered, should be located between the sand, cement and water so that mortar may be prepared — and the mixer cleaned afterwards — with the minimum of materials handling (Figure 20). The basic aim of good yard layout is to have everything ready to hand and easy to find — including handtools; clambering over stored materials to reach equipment is wasteful of time and materials.

Most of the above is, of course, just common sense and its value will be readily appreciated and recognized during the course of construction work.

(b) Formwork

Conventional ferrocement structures are built up by working mortar into several layers of wire mesh tied closely to a self-supporting frame of core rods. The design shown here uses only one or two layers of mesh and both mesh and mortar are laid onto formwork making construction simple and cheap. Evaporation is therefore reduced during the crucial first twenty-four hours after the mortar has been applied, as it takes place through one face only.

The formwork must be strong enough to take the strain of the tightened mesh and the weight of the wet mortar without

Figure 19.
Covered work area in
which tools, formwork,
sand, etc can be stored and
protected.

Figure 20.
Petrol engine-powered
mortar mixer on swivel
stand.

sagging or moving. It must be easy to erect and must be waterproofed to avoid absorbing water from the mortar, and slightly flexible to ease stripping. It must also be cheap to make and replace and easy to repair.

Many materials can be used to make the formwork, including steel, glass reinforced fibre, and plywood/timber. Angle iron and steel plate without doubt make the most durable and satisfactory forms, but these are expensive. Glass reinforced plastic (GRP) is easy to lay up on a mould, thereby making replacement forms simple to construct, but GRP is an expensive material. Plywood and timber formwork is simple to construct using handtools and its life can be extended considerably by reinforcing the joints with GRP; construction details for these forms are outlined in this chapter (see Figure 21).

Curved ribs for the wall formwork are drawn and cut out from 10mm plywood and nailed to 100 × 25mm wooden spars; the spars have thick sections in order to reduce their deflection when the plywood is fastened to them. Next, 4mm plywood is cut to size and tacked onto this frame, the edges are planed smooth and the joints reinforced with strips of GRP — using cheap glassfibre matting. The plywood does not need to be marine grade as it will be protected by the GRP. The formwork components are finally painted with GRP resin and allowed to dry. Construction details for these forms are shown in Figure 21; they may be made to any dimensions required. If they are looked after, cleaned after use and repaired when necessary, they should have a life lasting over 50 years. Between each pair of forms a timber wedge is bolted that is pulled out from inside during dismantling and formwork stripping.

The tank design described in this chapter has built-in partition walls made from thin slabs of mesh reinforced mortar; a cheaper design would construct block or brick walls inside the tank after installation which would be quite satisfactory but time-consuming. The moulds for the partition walls are shown in Figure 22. These are made from plywood sheet screwed to a stiff frame — old timber doors

Figure 21. Building the formwork from plywood.

(a) Cut out rib.

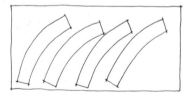

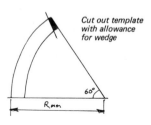

mark template on plywood
and cut out ribs

Cut out template
with allowance
for wedge

60°

R mm

(b) Assemble.

Screw
spars
to ribs

(c) Add plywood.

Screw and
glue plywood
sheet to ribs

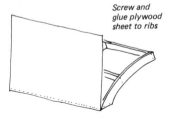

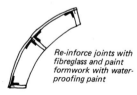

Re-inforce joints with
fibreglass and paint
formwork with water-
proofing paint

(d) Assemble.

Weage

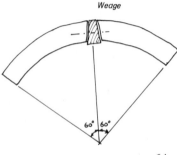

Assemble pairs of forms
with wedge, drill hole
through and bolt. Three
pairs of forms are used
for each tank

60° 60°

64

Figure 22. Mould for partition walls.

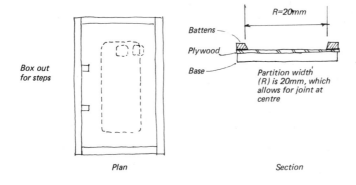

Box out
for steps

Battens

Plywood

Base

R=20mm

Partition width
(R) is 20mm, which
allows for joint at
centre

Plan

Section

Figure 23. Moulds for floor slab (6N°).

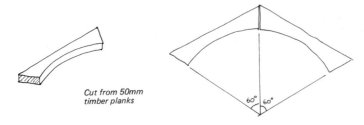

Cut from 50mm
timber planks

60° 60°

Figure 24. Roof shuttering (3N°).

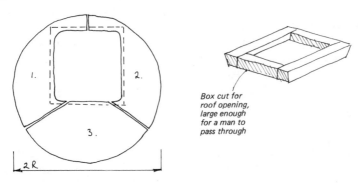

1.

2.

3.

2R

Box cut for
roof opening,
large enough
for a man to
pass through

are ideal for this — with wooden battens screwed on to make the mould edges. In this way thin slabs of widely differing shapes can be cast with cut-outs and box-outs wherever they are needed. The wooden battens are chamfered to prevent the slabs from sticking in the mould; the mould is also waterproofed using resin or varnish, although this quickly wears off during use.

Moulds for the floor slab are built up out of timber or plywood; those shown in Figure 23 are made from strips of plywood screwed together and cut to shape using a power jig saw. They are also waterproofed with resin. Moulds for the tank centre steps are cut out in the same way.

Finally, shuttering for the roof is made out of plywood (Figure 24). These need to fit well and be free from distortion otherwise the mortar applied to the top falls through the joints. It has been found that two sheets of plywood, cut to shape and separated by timber battens to make a 'box', are light and strong shutters. These are also waterproofed. The moulding for the manhole lip is constructed from timber sections with plywood corner gussets.

The formwork and moulds do not have to be made accurately to high tolerances or perfectly aligned during the construction work. One of the great advantages of ferrocement as a construction material is its tolerance to inaccurate workmanship; minor variations in shape are not important.

A release oil is applied to the formwork and moulds before use to prevent the mortar from sticking to them. Many proprietary oils are available and are equally successful; a thick oil or cream that may be brushed on is preferable to a thin oil as the former helps fill cracks in the forms. The life of the formwork depends very largely on the care with which the release oil is applied as 'stuck' forms usually have to be forced or cut to release them. They should be scrubbed clean with a stiff brush and water straight after stripping to prevent the build up of mortar layers.

(c) Materials
Thin shell structures such as septic tanks are not heavily loaded under normal conditions. Provided they are soundly

made with the correct reinforcement, plastered with a strong mortar, and provided they are correctly installed, the septic tanks described here will give a long and trouble-free life. Such has been the experience in New Zealand.

The requirements of sound construction are sound materials and good workmanship; a general specification of materials is given below as a basic guideline. In practice, the tanks have a large factor of safety of strength and the specification may be relaxed, but this should only be done after expert technical advice has been sought. A more comprehensive specification is given in the references.

Sand. The quality and grading of the sand for the mortar is of prime importance as it affects the strength and durability of the cured mortar. Sand is made up from many types of material, such as quartz, basalt, limestone or even soft coral; it must be resistant to abrasion and chemical attack and be non-porous. Sharp silica sands from water washed quartz make an excellent aggregate.

The grading of the sand should fall within Zone 2, Grade B, for fine aggregates, BS882, 1965. Correct grading is necessary to secure a workable mix that gives a dense, strong mortar; too much silt requires more water, with a corresponding reduction in strength whereas inadequate silt or 'fines' gives a coarse mix that is difficult to trowel. The table of sieve sizes (see below) and the percentage passing by weight defines Zone 2, Grade B, which lies between the percentage boundaries given.

To carry out this test a sample of the sand being analyzed is dried, weighed and placed in the top of the stack of sieves. The sieves are shaken until each sand particle has dropped to

	Sieve size (British Standard)	% passing BS sieve by weight
	7	75 - 100
	14	55 - 90
Grade B	25	35 - 59
	52	10 - 30
	100	0 - 10

the sieve that finally holds it, and the weight of sand retained on each sieve is measured. From this it is a simple step to calculate the percentage of sand by weight that is retained, and by subtraction the percentage weight that passes each sieve.

Many natural alluvial sands fall roughly within Zone 2. Sieves and weighing scales may not be available locally and a standard sand sample may be carried for the purposes of rough visual comparison.

The silt or clay content of the sand can be simply found by shaking a sample in a glass of water and allowing it to settle. Silt and clay particles that settle slowly will form a layer above the coarser particles — if these make up more than 10 per cent of the sample volume the sand must be either washed or abandoned. This simple test may be used to check a sand if sieves and scales are not available.

Cement. This binds the sand particles together and its quality and quantity determines the final strength of the mortar. It must be fresh, with no signs of caking or lumps: cement does not last long in humid climates after the bag has been opened. Correct storage has already been described. Occasional lumps can be sieved out of the cement, but if there are many lumps present it could mean that the cement has already 'aged' and begun to set. In this case the final mortar will be weak.

The cement should be ordinary Portland cement to BS12 or equivalent; slower setting sulphate-resisting cements may also be used but there is no real advantage in using these.

Water — must be free from suspended clays or dissolved organic matter — contaminated water gives a low strength mortar. Generally, water that is fit to drink will be suitable for concrete. The quantity of water used partly determines the final mortar strength.

Plasticizers improve the workability of the mortar and reduce the water content. A variety of products are commercially available to the building trade and mixing proportions and instructions should be carefully followed. Plasticizers are not expensive, and they make plastering simple, giving a dense, void-free mortar.

Plasticizers, to improve workability, are not usually recommended for ferrocement shells needing very high strengths — such as those required in boat construction, for instance. But in the tanks described here they make travelling easy and help the mortar to 'stick' on to the formwork.

Re-inforcement is needed to strengthen the mortar and provide some control over shrinkage cracking. In the design for the circular tank the wire wrapped around the tank is assumed to take the hoop tension loads; the stresses at the junctions between the wall, roof and base slab are carried by strips of wire mesh. Mesh is used primarily to control shrinkage cracking and provide a strong surface of the mortar shell against handling shocks.

Several types of mesh are used. Hexagonal 'chicken wire' from twisted soft iron wire is readily available and satisfactory — it is flexible but tends to distort out of shape. Stiffer welded square mesh from 19 gauge wire at 12mm centres is easier to lay onto the cylindrical walls, and tight corners may be reinforced by cutting strips of mesh and 'stitching' the overlaps together.

The hoop wire reinforcement should be from 3mm diameter cold drawn fencing wire; this wire is of great tensile strength.

Both the mesh and the hoop wire should be well galvanized to prevent them from corrosion should the mortar become cracked or damaged. On no account should aluminium painted wire be used, as the aluminium reacts with the cement giving a poor bond.

The mesh used for the thin cast panels, the base slab and the roof, must be flat and rigid enough to be pushed into the wet mortar. Suitable meshes are 25 × 25 × 3mm or 50 × 50 × 3mm, ungalvanized, mild steel.

(d) Mixing the mortar

The final strength of the shell depends on many factors — the grading of the sand, the amount and grade of cement used, the amount of water used in the mix, the degree of compaction achieved during plastering, the reinforcement used, and the method of curing. All these factors including the last are interrelated.

A coarse sand needs extra cement to make a workable mortar which increases the risk of shrinkage cracks; a silty sand needs extra water which reduces the strength of the mortar itself. A dense, compact, strong shell with no air voids requires a mortar mix that is workable yet not too wet. It is best to keep the ratio of cement and sand constant during the mixing operation and achieve good workability by varying water content up to the maximum limit.

Cement:sand ratio (by volume). Experience has shown that a mix using one part by volume of cement to 2½ parts by volume of dry sand provides a satisfactory mix that is easy to work. Weaker mixes were tried but these did not set hard enough for the forms to be stripped out the next day. The volumes should be scaled using a bucket or box — estimating volumes on a shovel is a totally inadequate method of measurement and should under no circumstances be allowed.

Water:cement ratio (by weight). Provided the mortar can be fully compacted the drier the mix the greater the final mortar strength; dry mixes are, however, difficult to plaster and fatiguing to compact. Wet, creamy mixes are easy to plaster in thin layers but have lower strength and durability after curing. A compromise must be made between a strong dry mix that is difficult to work and compact; and a wet, creamy mix that is easy to apply yet weak when cured. The ratio of water:cement should not exceed the value of 0.45 at which point the cured strength begins to decline drastically.

In practice, water is added to the mix until it looks workable enough for use — this condition is not difficult to judge from experience. A trial mix is made up using cement and *dry* sand to the ratio of 1:2½ (by volume); the weight of cement used is therefore known. Water, mixed with plasticizer, is scaled and mixed into the cement and sand until a workable mix is reached and the ratio of cement:water (by weight) is calculated. This should not exceed the value

0.45-0.50; if it does, then a better grade of sand should be sought or a greater cement:sand ratio should be used. Several trial mixes made up in this way using the available sand allow the people engaged in the mixing to get the feel of a satisfactory mix.

(e) Machine mixing

Most text books on ferrocement indicate that the mortar can only be satisfactorily mixed in a motorized pan or paddle type mixer, the argument being that the conventional horizontal drum mixer cannot handle the drier mixes needed for ferrocement work. The drum mixer is, however, many times cheaper than the pan mixer, more readily available, and is quite satisfactory.

A design mix is chosen and the cement, sand, water and plasticizer scaled ready. About two thirds of the water with mixed plasticizer is added to the rotating drum and the cement tipped in. When this is thoroughly mixed to a lump-free slurry the scaled sand is gradually added until the mortar mass falls at each revolution of the drum in a smooth surfaced plastic lump. The rest of the sand is then gradually added, the workability of the mortar being kept steady by adding small volumes of the remaining water; it will be found that small volumes of water make a large difference to workability which also increases with time of mixing. Usually the sand will contain some water from storage. Samples of the mortar may be taken from the drum and turned over by a trowel on a board — a good workable mortar will stand up with little slumping yet have a creamy solid surface and shape with no crumbling. Plasterers quickly learn what a good workable mortar looks like as they are the ones who have to lay it on.

The period of mixing should not exceed three or four minutes otherwise air becomes entrapped in the mortar and its strength and watertightness are reduced. An insufficiently mixed mortar, on the other hand, will be lumpy and difficult to use.

There are several tests used in large scale concrete construction yards to test the workability of concrete mixes;

one of these is the standard slump test with the vertical, open ended cone which is recommended for high quality ferrocement work. Although this test is useful it is not needed for the small batch mortar mixes used in septic tank construction — provided the plasterers are experienced.

Table 6. List of tools needed.

1 set of forms for walls, roof, floor (the most expensive item)
1 mortar mixer
1 wheelbarrow
3 shovels
3 steel floats
3 mortar hawks
2 bolt cutters for thick mesh
2 wire snips
2 pincers
1 tape measure
3 measuring buckets paint brushes, tie wire, mould oil etc. First Aid Kit

A running check may also be kept on mortar quality by taking occasional samples in a 50 × 50mm mould, curing them under water for 28 days, then crushing them to destruction. The compressive strength should exceed 42 Newtons/cu mm, (6,000 lb/sq in). This test needs a laboratory and gives results a month after the mortar has been used to build a tank. It provides some form of quality control but the best form of quality control is experienced and conscientious plasterers.

(f) Tools

A list of tools needed is given in Table 6 and the numbers given refer to those needed for a small construction yard employing three or four people. The tools should be returned to a safe, convenient place at the end of each working day

Figure 25. Constructing partition walls.

Figure 25a.
Lay ungalvanized weld mesh over mould and cut to shape.

Figure 25b.
*Wood blocks used for box-outs with mesh cut to shape. In this picture
the blocks are shown removable, which helps stripping.*

73

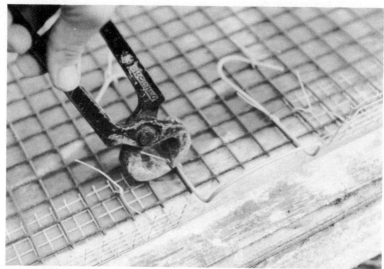

Figure 25c.
Handles made from 2.5mm fencing wire tied to weld mesh. In this picture 19mm weld mesh is shown as edge reinforcement — but this is not needed.

Figure 25d.
Brush mould well with release oil.

Figure 25e.
Fill mould with mortar, and spread using steel float from centre.

Figure 25f.
Place cut weld mesh onto mortar in mould.

75

after cleaning and oiling; a tool rack on a wall is a handy addition to a yard.

A small, powered-drum concrete-mixer is a must for the mortar mixing and its use has already been described. Small portable, petrol-driven mixers that swivel on a stand are ideal as they can be turned around for washing down and for tipping the mortar into a wheelbarrow for delivery to the tanks under construction.

4 CONSTRUCTION DETAILS

(a) Casting the partition walls

The partition walls in this design are pre-cast (see Figure 25) and built into the tanks when the cylindrical walls are constructed; alternatively the partitions may be built on site using blocks or bricks after the tank has been installed in the excavation — this makes the tank lighter to carry and cheaper.

When the tank is full, the sewage level in each compartment will be equal, so the partition walls do not take any load, but they need to be reinforced and strengthened for handling and erection. 20mm thick panels reinforced with 25 × 25 × 3mm ungalvanized weld mesh can be stripped from the moulds and erected after only 24 hours curing. If the curing period is longer and the mortar allowed to harden the 50 × 50 × 3mm mesh will be sufficient.

The ungalvanized weld mesh reinforcement, which should have been stored flat to avoid bends, is laid over the mould and cut with the bolt cutters to leave a 25mm gap between the mesh and the inside edges of the mould timber battens (Figure 25a). The mesh is also cut around the box-outs in the panels (Figure 25b). Wire handles are tied to this reinforcement using thin, soft iron tie wire (Figure 25c).

This mould is brushed all over with release oil, both inside and over the timber battens to prevent the mortar from sticking (Figure 25d). Mortar is then shovelled into the centre of the mould and worked by steel float with few strokes to the edges, filling the mould. The mortar is 'rolled' and pressed across the mould face rather than pushed to avoid rubbing the release oil off the mould face (Figure 25e). With practice the amount of mortar needed to fill the mould can be judged and steel-floated quickly without leaving voids or air bubbles. The mortar is screed off level with the top of the battens, low spots being made up. On no account should the mortar be trowelled or be applied in layers — the steel float brings cement slurry to the surface which provides a very poor bond with the next layer.

Small pads of scrap weld mesh from $12 \times 12 \times 19$ gauge mesh are folded into 7mm thick layers and pressed into the mortar to the mould face at 300mm centres; these are spacers which maintain the mesh reinforcement position and cover. The weld mesh, previously cut to shape, is then pressed into the mortar until it reaches the spacers (Figure 25fg), at which point it will be in the centre of the mortar layer; the wire handles are bent up over the timber battens. The mortar is then worked backwards and forwards with the steel float until the reinforcement is covered and the surface is smooth (Figure 25h).

The partition mould is then left for twenty-four hours or more under cover or until it is ready for stripping. As soon as the mortar is brush hard, it is sealed with a coat of PVA diluted to the ratio 1:3 (1 part PVA:3 parts water by volume), or covered with plastic sheeting or wet sacking. It is essential that the loss of water be prevented during the early stages of curing, or shrinkage cracking takes place which seriously weakens the structure. Partitions cast in this way are stripped by tilting the mould on edge to a vertical position and carefully prising the wall casting loose by pulling on the wire handles; the edges can be shaken free by hitting the wooden battens with a block of wood and hammer. Partitions have been stripped and erected after only twenty-four hours but in this condition the mortar is 'green' and has low strength; leaving the castings to harden for several days allows them to shrink and be easily lifted from the tilted mould, but then the mould cannot be used. On no account should the panels be carried except on their edges; they should also be stored on their edges, both sides painted with dilute PVA.

(b) Casting the tank base

The concrete construction pad is covered with a plastic sheet

Figure 25g.
Press mesh into mortar layer until it reaches pads of scrap mesh already pressed down to mould base.

Figure 25h.
Work mortar layer by steel float to give smooth surface, then screed level with a timber batten.

and the oiled base forms assembled and fastened together (see Figure 26a). Two sheets of 25 × 25 × 3mm weld mesh are fastened along their long edges with a 50mm overlap and laid over the circle made by the base forms. The mesh is cut to give a 25mm gap all round to the inside edge of the forms, then it is lifted out and three wire hoops bent and tied onto the underside of the mesh; these hooks are used to lift the tanks and are made from 4 strands of 3mm wire tied and twisted together (Figure 26b).

The slab is designed so that the mesh is in the upper half of the section to provide resistance to cracking due to uneven excavation. This might cause puncture failure. Small pre-cast mortar spacer blocks 25mm thick are placed inside the base form to support the partition walls and mesh (Figure 26c).

The base form is then filled with mortar and screeded level, care being taken not to disturb the spacer blocks. Strips of galvanized 12 × 12 × 19 gauge weld mesh, 150mm wide by 300mm long are pressed into the mortar around the edges of the base leaving a 150mm overlap on the base forms. These strips are pressed down to the bottom of the mortar layer; the pre-cut weld mesh is placed on the mortar surface and it is also pressed down until it reaches the spacer blocks. The mortar is worked smooth again with a steel float in the way already described.

As soon as the mortar has hardened sufficiently the loose forms are stripped and the slab is covered to prevent rapid drying and cracking. At this stage it is useful to work out the lines of the partition walls and the centre point of the base into the soft mortar.

(c) Erecting partition walls and wall formwork

The partition walls are carried on edge to the base slab and carefully positioned on the previously marked out lines (Figure 27a). A simple jig can be employed to hold the partition in position at the top; this jig also ensures that the walls divide the base slab exactly into three equal segments (Figure 27b). The pre-cast discs of mortar that make steps down the centre of the tank are inserted into the central joint of the walls as they are positioned. The partitions are checked for verticality by a spirit level.

Figure 26. Casting the base slab.

Figure 26a.
Base moulds on plastic sheeting.

Figure 26b.
Wire hoops fastened and bent to shape to provide lifting hoops.

Figure 26c.
Small, 25mm thick mortar pads cast in base, supporting mesh reinforcement.

The formwork for the outer walls is now bolted loosely together with the forms in pairs and the wedge in the centre and coated with release oil (Figure 27c). Each pair of forms is carried to the base slab and positioned in the three segments made by the partition walls. The base slab should protrude slightly from under the formwork. At this stage it may be necessary to adjust the partition walls to provide a good fit with the wall formwork. A circle of 3mm fencing wire is passed around the forms 25mm from the top and the bottom to hold them together and twisted tight. Gaps in the formwork can be plugged full of newspaper to prevent the mortar from being pushed through; if this is not done then the forms may be difficult to free when stripping.

The strips of 12 × 12 × 19 gauge weld mesh from the base slab are folded up around the wall forms and tied flat with another circle of 3mm wire (Figure 27d).

The walls are now ready to be plastered.

(d) Plastering the walls

A 5mm thick layer of mortar is trowelled onto the wall forms. If the mortar is too wet it will slump off — if too dry, it will be difficult to work. It is best to begin plastering from the bottom of the walls, working each float-load of mortar upwards then sideways around the tank. The mortar is placed on a 'spot' board at the base of the wall, a float-load is lifted onto a hawk then transferred back to the float for plastering. The spot board catches any falling mortar and prevents dirt and rubbish from being mixed in. Small loads should be used — if too much is plastered then the layer becomes too heavy and rolls off. With practice one man can plaster a layer over a complete tank in about half an hour (Figure 28a). The mortar is carefully pressed and worked into the base so that no voids are left between the wall shell and base slab, and pressed through the base slab mesh folded and tied to the wall. At the top of the tank the mortar is cut off level with the top of the wall forms around the tank.

Mesh is now cut to length to be wrapped around the tank with a 150mm overlap. If mesh rolls 1m wide are used then two strips are necessary. The length is best measured directly by wrapping a string around the tank and finding its actual circumference.

The mesh is coiled at each end, carried to the tank, and unwrapped and pulled closely around the tank; this operation takes two people. It is tied together at the overlap using soft iron tie wire and the mesh crimped tight using long nosed pliers. Crimping is best achieved in vertical rows up the tank wall by first pulling a 'ridge' out before the ridge is crimped tight using the pincers (Figure 28b). The second layer of mesh is wrapped around the top half of the tank leaving a 150mm overlap at the top. It is fastened and crimped tight in a similar manner. These layers of mesh will bite into the first layer of mortar but not so far as to reach the surface of the forms. Tying on the mesh takes about one hour.

The hoop wire is now wrapped around the tank in a spiral, with 25mm spacings in the bottom half and 50mm spacings in the top half (Figure 28c). The wire is first hooked at the end and tied flat to the mesh before it is unreeled and pulled tight around the tank. Again, two people are needed for this

Figure 27. Erecting partition walls and wall forms.

Figure 27a.
*Erecting the partition walls
— in this picture the base
has not yet been cast.*

Figure 27b.
Simple jig used to hold tops of partition walls in position.

Figure 27c.
Bolting pairs of wall forms together with wedge in between.

Figure 27d.
Wall forms in position. Lifting hook is shown under the partition wall. Forms are first held by a loop of wire tied tightly; then the base weld mesh is bent up and tied tightly against the oiled forms.

operation, one unreeling and the other pulling the wire tight and keeping the spacing accurate. Unreeling the wire is better than simply pulling it off the side of the coil as this prevents kinks and knots in the wire, which makes this part of the job exceptionally difficult. The wire, if it runs out before it reaches the top of the tank, may be hooked and tied flat to the mesh; a new coil is started giving a 150mm overlap. The wire hoops are twisted using pliers to ensure that the wire is tightened onto the mesh beneath at all points (Figure 28d). About 10kg of 2.5mm fencing wire is needed for this work which in fact provides a major part of the shell hoop reinforcement. This operation takes half an hour.

A second mortar layer 10mm thick is now applied to the walls in the same way described above and worked into the mesh. Its thickness is carefully maintained over the tank walls especially at the top edge where it is cut off level all round using the steel float.

The thickness of the wall should now be approximately 15mm and this may be checked by pushing a piece of tie wire through to the formwork.

A second layer of weld mesh, 12 × 12 × 19 gauge, is now fastened and tightened onto the tank walls. This second layer is not absolutely necessary for it is an expensive material to use and time consuming to fix, but provides a surface on which the final mortar layer can be applied to give a smooth finish. Tanks made without this second layer have proved perfectly satisfactory in practice.

A final layer of mortar 5mm thick is plastered onto the walls and worked level. When the mortar has begun to stiffen and set it can be wetted and worked to a smooth, shiny surface to give a pleasing appearance to the finished tank.

The finished walls will have a thickness of 20-25mm, with mesh at each face to provide strength against shrinkage cracks. The mortar at the top is cut level with the formwork and, when the mortar has hardened sufficiently, the walls are painted with the diluted PVA to prevent loss of moisture and aid curving. After twenty-four hours the formwork is ready for stripping.

Figure 28. Laying on wall mortar.

Figure 28a.
Laying on the first mortar layer with a steel float; a rough finish is quite satisfactory as mesh will be pressed into it. Note how the mortar has been well worked into the base under the forms. In this picture partition wall reinforcement is shown protruding.

Figure 28b.
Crimping the wall mesh tight with long-nosed pliers. The loose mesh is first pulled out as shown, then the ridge is crimped tight and the fold bent down.

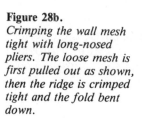

86

Figure 28c.
Galvanized fencing wire is wound round the tank over first layer of weld mesh.

Figure 28d.
Hoop wire is tightened by twisting wire with pliers. Note how wet mortar is forced through mesh layer.

(e) Stripping the formwork

Stripping the formwork should under no account be delayed beyond twenty-four hours. The mortar shell shrinks as it sets and binds the edges of the forms making them difficult to dismantle.

The timber wedges are first unbolted and taken out from between each pair of forms; if stuck they can be knocked in from outside. Each form is then tugged inwards until it is loose and comes away from the wall. If the middle edges of each pair of forms are trapped by a lip of mortar pushed into the form/wedge joint, this lip may be cut away carefully with a chisel (Figure 29a). After twenty-four hours the mortar is still green and plastic and care must be taken when tugging on the forms that the wall does not twist excessively and crack.

Each form is stripped in turn and lifted out of the tank for cleaning. Broken mortar fragments are brushed up and removed from the tank floor and the inside wall/floor joint painted with diluted PVA; the top edge of the mortar is also painted to provide a bond with the roof (Figure 29b).

It is now time to construct the roof.

(f) Constructing the roof

The roof shutters are oiled and placed on props leant inside each segment of the tank (Figure 30a). These props are adjusted so that the shutters are level with the top of the mortar wall. A jig to form the manhole is now either bolted or clamped into place (Figure 30b).

Weld mesh, 25 × 25 × 3mm is tied together in the same way described for the base slab and cut to shape to fit the roof. The reinforcement in this case should extend to the galvanized mesh reinforcement protruding up out of the walls. The wall mesh strips are bent down to the roof shutter and 7mm thick pads of mesh made to provide spacers for the roof reinforcement. Any gaps between the roof shutters and walls may be filled with newspaper or wedges of rolled weld mesh — gaps of up to 30mm have been successfully bridged in this way to prevent the roof mortar from slumping down. If the wall reinforcing strips are difficult to fasten down they

Figure 29a. Stripping wall forms.

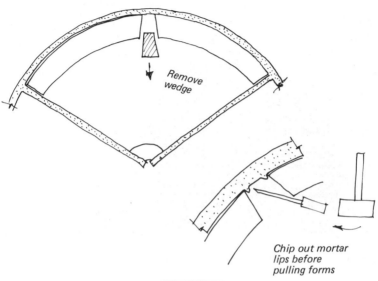

Remove wedge

Chip out mortar
lips before
pulling forms

**Figure 29b. Inside view of
tank with forms stripped.**
*Mesh overlap at top cut
and folded outwards; the
mortar is painted with
dilute PVA. Note cut-outs
for liquor to flow into the
last compartment before
discharge.*

Figure 30. Constructing roof of tank.

Figure 30a.
Roof shutters propped up from below and ready to be positioned.

Figure 30b.
*Roof shutters in position, with manhole form held in place by 'G' clamp.
Note gap between shutters and the partition walls compared with strips
of weld mesh to hold mortar in place.*

90

may be folded and tied onto the roof mesh after the roof mesh and mortar have been placed.

The roof is plastered with 30mm of mortar and screeded level. The spacers are pushed into the mortar to the shutters, and the reinforcing mesh lifted up and pressed into place. The mortar surface is again worked smooth and the gaps filled. An accurate roof/wall edge corner can be made by wrapping a strip of rubber belting or steel sheet around the tank and plastering up against it. The mortar at the top edge of the walls must be well worked in to obtain a good watertight joint.

If a lip is required around the manhole this may be made by first roughing the wet surface of the mortar, laying on oiled battens, and filling the gap up to the manhole jig. The wood battens are pulled off the roof after the roof has set.

After twenty-four hours the props are pulled out and the roof shutters carefully pulled down and taken out. The roof is painted with dilute PVA which is also worked into the vertical joint between the three partition walls.

The tank is again cleaned of loose mortar and dust and is ready for the final finishing work.

(g) Finishing work

Finishing work consists basically of plastering fillets of mortar into the joints to strengthen them and cover any exposed wires. The two hoop wires used initially to tighten up the wall forms must be covered by the fillets. The dry coat of PVA provides a good bond between mortar layers. Mortar may be applied using a small diamond shaped trowel or worked on by hand — if the mortar is reasonably stiff there will be no difficulties in making up the joints. The fillets should be small to avoid adding too much weight to the tank.

(h) Pipework

At this stage holes are cut into the mortar walls for the inlet and outlet pipes whilst the mortar is still green. A hammer and cold chisel are needed for this task. The positions of the holes are marked out taking care to ensure that the inlet pipe into the larger first chamber is 25mm higher than the outlet

Figure 31. Cutting holes for pipework.
The mortar is 'green' and easy to chisel out with a blunt wood chisel.

from the smaller second chamber. The mortar is broken away in layers starting from the outside of the marked out circles (Figure 31). When the mesh is reached it is cut radially and each segment folded back; the hoop wire is cut and removed by using the bolt cutters. With care an accurate hole can be made with little overbreak and damage to the surrounding mortar and the pipework will make a tight fit.

Several types of pipework can be fitted but the final choice must depend on the pipework used locally for sewerage work. Construction is made simple if a pipe connector is built into the wall that can later be connected to sewerage pipework and the internal fittings. Plastic connections are light and cheap and were used in the design described here.

The fittings are inserted through the holes, adjusted for line and level — the inlet pipe must be 25mm above the level of the outlet pipe — the wire mesh is bent against the fittings and the gap mortared solid from both sides. This mortar collar is built up to provide a solid support for the fitting to prevent it from shearing off if settlement occurs in the ground.

The outlet pipe may be taken through the tank wall on the opposite side to the inlet pipe by cutting a hole in the partition wall. This may be preferred for connections on site and is satisfactory if carefully made.

(i) Casting the manhole cover slab

One of the advantages of using septic tanks to this design is that they can be de-sludged by hand — if this should ever prove necessary. The manhole walls to ground level are built up using bricks or precast concrete sections and the top covered with a cover slab. The slab of this particular tank design had cast within it a galvanized iron manhole cover and an air vent in order to conform to the local Building Regulations.

A simpler, cheaper, design would use a plain reinforced concrete slab over the manhole which could be removed whenever required.

Figure 32. Delivery of tanks.
Use of hydraulic crane on lorry shown.

93

(j) Curing the tank

The tank is now filled with 25mm or so of water, the manhole covered, and allowed to cure for two weeks before removal. Tanks have, however, been constructed and installed within three days with no resulting damage.

5 DELIVERY AND INSTALLATION

Delivery. Ferrocement septic tanks are heavy and have to be delivered on a trailer. Weighing around 1 tonne, they are lifted by machine or tackle using three strong ropes tied one to each lifting strap; the lifting ropes should be protected with padding at the top of the tank (see Figure 32). Delivery is made simple and speedy if a lorry equipped with a hydraulic crane is available (Figure 32). In this case the tank may be taken to difficult sites and lowered to the other side of walls and ditches. Alternatively the tank may be propped up on skids and winched onto a low loading trailer for delivery; at the site it is simply winched off again.

Installation. The site for the tank and soakaway is selected according to the principles described in Chapter 2. A trial excavation pit should be constructed at the tank site to check that rock will not prevent digging; if rock or wet and difficult conditions are met then the tank site can be changed (Figure 33a). Generally the cost of extra sewerage pipe work is small compared with the costs of excavation in bad ground. Contractors are usually well aware of the risks and losses that may occur with underground works.

If the trial excavation is satisfactory then the sewerage pipe work trench is excavated to the tank site at the correct slope — usually not less than 1 in 50. Excavation continues at the tank site until the bottom is 1.50m below the base of the pipe trench — this allows the pipe work to directly run to the inlet pipe on the tank (Figure 33b).

A 100mm layer of sand or fine gravel is bedded into the base of the excavation and screeded level (Figure 33c), the tank is lowered into position and aligned and the ropes unfastened (Figure 33d). The space around the excavation is backfilled in 150mm layers which are carefully compacted by

Figure 33. Tank installation.

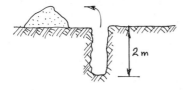

(a) Trial excavation of tank site. Check for rock or running sand.

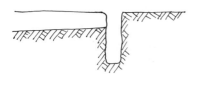

(b) Excavate trench from soakage area to tank site.

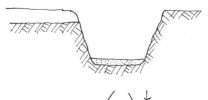

(c) Excavate pit for tank, lay 100 mm layer of sand in base of pit.

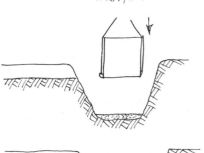

(d) Lower tank into pit, line up pipe fittings to trench.

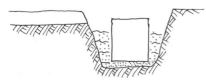

(e) Backfill in 150 mm layers; compact each layer.

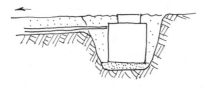

(f) Connect pipework, erect manhole, and backfill to surface.

treading underfoot — if the soil is dry it may have to be dampened to aid compaction (Figure 33e). If compaction is inadequate settlement will occur over the months and the pipework will settle and either fracture or pull out of joint.

The pipe work is laid in the trench on screeded gravel and connected to the tank. The slope of the pipe work should be carefully maintained to ensure the free flow of the sewage. Outlet pipe work is also connected up, the manhole is built and the excavation backfilled to the surface (Figure 33f).

If ground water seeps into the excavation it may be pumped or bucketted out. It is possible to lower a ferrocement tank into a flooded excavation provided that the gravel base is at the correct level and has been screeded, and provided that the surrounding ground is firm enough to support the machine. Wet ground should, however, be avoided.

Complete septic tank systems have been installed, including pipe work, manholes and soakaway, in less than a day by two men and a machine.

6 POTENTIAL OF FERROCEMENT FOR THIN SHELL SANITATION STRUCTURES

The ferrocement septic tank described above was developed for rural areas in Britain where prefabricated tanks have found favour over in-situ constructed tanks — mainly because of the speed of installation. The design is expensive and therefore has little relevance to low income communities, except in the circumstances discussed in Chapter 1. However, the design is capable of much modification and simplification.

Ferrocement is strong and durable, needs no expensive machines for construction and is highly labour-intensive. It is easy for use by semi-skilled workers and many of the skills are often locally known. Ferrocement tanks are lighter than cast concrete tanks yet they are too heavy to manhandle — they must be delivered to the site on a trailer and lowered into the excavation by machine or lifting tackle. Although simple, construction work must be carefully carried out if the tank is to be watertight.

Among the sanitation options described in Chapter 1, ferrocement may be used advantageously in the construction of aqua-privies, septic tanks, and vaults — structures whose main requirement is that they be watertight. Small aqua-privies may be built using the bare minimum of expensive mesh — if indeed mesh is needed at all; glass fibre strands may be used to provide alternative shrinkage resistance and corner reinforcement. The aqua-privies may have a removable slab lid which will allow an internal partition wall to be constructed and improve the settling efficiency of the tank.

Septic tanks for larger communities allow the high initial cost to be shared, and are used where land is available for effluent disposal, or where secondary and tertiary treatment is employed before the effluent is discharged to a water course. The design shown in this chapter may be simplified by constructing the partition walls on site out of blocks and fitting the pipework lower down the walls which removes the need for the manhole structure on top.

Vaults for sewage storage made from ferrocement may be simple storage tanks whose design is described in the author's previous handbook (see Watt, 1978).

Ferrocement is a versatile material that can be used for a wide variety of products. Its value will be apparent in national economies where labour is still relatively cheap compared to capital, and where the industries making fibreglass, spun concrete pipes, etc. are not well established. The success of the ferrocement industry in New Zealand, by any account a high-income economy, suggests that its value is recognized for other partly industrialized countries.

References and Sources of Information

BS 882, 1201 (1965). *Aggregates from natural sources for concrete (including granolithic) Part 1: Imperial Units.* British Standards Institution, London.

BS 12 (1978). *Specifications for ordinary and rapid-hardening Portland cement.* British Standards Institution, London.

CP 302 (1972). *Small Sewage Treatment Works.* British Standards Institution, London. Succeeded by BS 6297 (1983).

ITDG (1979). *A Chinese Biogas Manual,* A. van Buren (ed.), I.T. Publications, London.

Maitra, M.S. (1978). 'Sanitation for the Poor in Calcutta', in *Sanitation in Developing Countries,* John Wiley and Sons.

Pickford, J. (1980). *The Design of Septic Tanks and Aqua Privies,* Overseas Building Notes No.187, Building Research Establishment, Overseas Division.

U.S. D.H.E.W. (1959). *Manual of Septic-Tank Practice,* U.S. Department of Health, Education and Welfare. Public Health Service Publication No.526.

Watt, S.B. (1978). *Ferrocement Water Tanks and their Construction,* I.T. Publications, London.

WEDC, 1979. *Chamber capacities of septic tanks and aqua-privies, Phase 1 Report,* Waste and Water Engineering for Developing Countries (WEDC), and Building Research Establishment Report (Unpublished).

World Bank (1980). *Appropriate Technology for Water Supply and Sanitation,* Volumes 1-12, Transportation, Water and Telecommunications Department, The World Bank, Washington, D.C.

World Bank (1980a). Vol.1a. *A Summary of Technical and Economic Options,* J.M. Kalbermatten, DeAnne S. Julius, and C.G. Gunnerson.

World Bank (1980b). *A Sanitation Field Manual,* Vol.11, J.M. Kalbermatten, DeAnne S. Julius, and C.G. Gunnerson.

98